Kaleigh,
    I was real
got the chance to talk
with you and your
sisters this weekend about
what I'd like to do for you
young ladies.
    I like the fact that you
speak your mind, you remind
me of me. yeah it gets me
in trouble some times but
hey I've made it this far
I'll be 53 in Sept on the
1st ♡

    So next year as a junior
talk to your advisor on where you
want to attend after high school

SIMPLE ACTS

OF

KINDNESS

500+ Ways to Make a Difference

ADAMS MEDIA

NEW YORK   LONDON   TORONTO   SYDNEY   NEW DELHI

Adams Media
An Imprint of Simon & Schuster, Inc.
57 Littlefield Street
Avon, Massachusetts 02322

First Adams Media hardcover edition OCTOBER 2017

ADAMS MEDIA and colophon are trademarks of Simon and Schuster.

For information about special discounts for bulk purchases, please contact Simon & Schuster Special Sales at 1-866-506-1949 or business@simonandschuster.com.

The Simon & Schuster Speakers Bureau can bring authors to your live event. For more information or to book an event contact the Simon & Schuster Speakers Bureau at 1-866-248-3049 or visit our website at www.simonspeakers.com.

Interior design by Colleen Cunningham
Interior images © 123RF/Olha Khomenko, Elena Paletskaya

Manufactured in the United States of America

10 9 8 7 6 5 4 3 2 1

Library of Congress Cataloging-in-Publication Data has been applied for.

ISBN 978-1-5072-0567-9
ISBN 978-1-5072-0568-6 (ebook)

Contains material adapted from the following title published by Adams Media, an Imprint of Simon & Schuster, Inc.: *The Nice Handbook* by Ruth Peterson, copyright © 2014, ISBN 978-1-4405-7354-5.

Introduction

Every day offers a new opportunity to be kind. Whether for a friend, a neighbor, coworker, or even Mother Earth, you'll never regret taking the time to show someone you care. *Simple Acts of Kindness* shares easy ways to add compassion, love, and gratitude to your day—and into the days of the people around you, including:

- Mowing your neighbor's yard
- Preparing a hot drink for your letter carrier in winter
- Bringing your dog to visit residents at a senior center
- Doing laundry for a new mother in your community
- Writing a thank-you note to a helpful coworker
- Leading a neighborhood recycling program
- Giving up your window seat to another passenger

And the generosity doesn't stop there—by simply being kind, you'll jump-start a ripple effect of good deeds. You'll find that when you go out of your way to brighten someone else's day, you'll also inspire friends, family, and even strangers to do nice things for others in their lives. When a friend sees you donating books to a local school, she may be inspired to volunteer to read at story hour. When a neighbor notices you shoveling snow for the older lady next door, the next time he heads to the grocery store he'll remember to check in and see if he can pick up some items for her.

Whether you only have five minutes to make someone's day or you're looking for a long-term way to make a major difference, flip through these pages and head out the door to start spreading kindness.

Make a treat to cheer up a gloomy Monday. It could be a healthy snack or a decadent dessert to enjoy with a hot cup of tea. Any little treat on a Monday can spark *kindness* that lasts the whole week.

● ● ●

Help set up a school's computer lab. Contact your local school and put your technological know-how to use. Most schools do not have an in-house IT professional, so by *volunteering* you're helping children's education and saving the school system money.

● ● ●

Recycle used plastic grocery store bags. If you forget to bring your reusable bag with you to the grocery store, don't feel too bad taking plastic—as long as you bring it back to the store's bag recycling box later!

Drive an elderly neighbor to a doctor's appointment. Getting to and from appointments may seem mundane to healthy, young, energetic individuals, but it can be a major headache for an elderly person without easy and accessible *transportation*.

●●●

DROP BY A FRIEND'S HOUSE WITH ICED COFFEE.

Clean up your language.
It's easy to fall into the habit
of using profanity, and it
sounds anything but *kind*
to those around you.

Show a *kid* how to ride a bicycle. Bike riding is a wonderful activity for children that gets them out in the fresh air. However, it can be a scary thing to learn how to do. Help your child or a neighborhood child learn how to pedal, steer, and brake her bike without her training wheels. Make sure she's wearing the proper helmet and pads before you do.

●●●

Place a love note somewhere hidden. Stick it inside his lunch bag, wallet, or jacket pocket. It is sure to inspire a *smile* when he unexpectedly discovers it.

●●●

Adopt an acre of vital wetlands. The African wetlands are in danger. Your *support* can help save these important migration areas. Check out www.awf.org to learn more about this type of geographical area and what you can do to save it.

Help those impacted by natural disasters.
Donate to the latest natural disaster relief fund via
local or national organizations in your country.
Your donation—be it time, goods, or money—will be of
great help to the thousands of families whose lives
have been turned upside down by a natural disaster.

● ● ●

Start a community garden. Get members of
your neighborhood and community to come
together for this beautifying and *eco-friendly*
endeavor. It creates green space in cities and gives
gardeners a way to share the land, their skills, and
their bounty with their community.

● ● ●

DONATE TO AN AREA MUSEUM.

9

Send a *bouquet* on
a random day.

Organize a *creativity* swap. Trade art materials with fellow artists, books with book lovers and writers, kitchen tools with friends who cook, and gardening seed and equipment with fellow gardeners. Why buy when you can swap! You'll share your materials and your passion.

●●●

GIVE SOMEONE A GIFT– JUST BECAUSE.

●●●

Orchestrate a spa day for your favorite girlfriends. Have it at your house. Arrange to have a manicurist, a massage therapist, and a hair and makeup expert come and teach you how to correctly do your nails, or your hair and makeup, and *enjoy* a massage.

Round up when you check out. Sometimes stores will have fundraising programs where you can round up your purchase price, donating the difference in change to a charity such as Autism Speaks. Even though it's less than a dollar, if everyone checking out at the store takes part, it can make a *big difference* to that organization.

●●●

Keep your grocery shopping *green*.
Buy fresh foods and eggs in cardboard containers—avoid Styrofoam.

●●●

Be frugal with water while brushing your teeth. Rinse to get the brush wet and rinse to clean the brush when you have finished brushing. Don't leave the water running the whole time. Use only what you need. You'll soon *discover* that you don't really need much water to brush.

Help an at-risk teen go to college. Work with other professionals in your community to assist an at-risk youth who may have the *intelligence* to do well in college but not understand the process or know how to find the resources to make it happen. You can make a difference in this person's life.

●●●

Write a *thank-you* note to a coworker. The next time he helps you with a project or a problem show your appreciation. A simple "thank you" might do, but a note shows your appreciation at a whole new level.

●●●

Donate books to schools. Look at your bookshelf and ask yourself if you're really ever going to reread each one. Schools can put used books to *good use* either through their loan system or by selling them at a used book sale and putting the profits toward buying new books.

Give a card to celebrate a child's achievement. Find a blank card or make a card and inscribe it with a message celebrating a child's act of *kindness*, athletic achievement, good grades—whatever! Kids love getting their own cards.

● ● ●

Become a global pen pal. Visit Global Penfriends (www.globalpenfriends.com) to find a *new friend* to correspond with.

● ● ●

Purchase beauty products that do not test on animals. When buying cosmetics or other beauty items, check the packaging or the manufacturer's website to ensure *kindness* to our animal friends.

Do laundry for a new mother. New parents are often overwhelmed, so why not show them some *kindness*? If a friend has recently had a baby, offer to wash, dry, and fold her clothes. Then cook her a meal before heading home!

Volunteer at your child's school.
Offer to drive on a field trip, work in the library, or serve as a teacher's aide. There are plenty of small jobs that can be a *big help* to teachers. Volunteer even if you don't have a child in school.

● ● ●

Opt for a ceramic mug rather than Styrofoam cup. Bring a mug to the office so you can use a *reusable* cup rather than waste a disposable one. Ask your manager if the company would purchase a new mug for everyone so Styrofoam will be obsolete in your office.

● ● ●

Give gifts to a needy family during the holidays.
Rather than exchanging gifts between family members, organize a drive for gifts to be donated to a needy family. You can either collect the actual gifts, or ask that family members donate the amount of money they would have spent on purchasing family gifts. What better time to spread *kindness* than the holidays!

Support literacy programs.
Teach a child or an illiterate person to read.
It will change their lives for the *better* and
you'll be earning some good karma. Check
https://proliteracy.org for more information.

• • •

Play a part in protecting the oceans' reefs.
Pledge money to save a specific area of these
underwater wonders and receive a deed to the reef
section you are personally *protecting*. Visit
www.savenature.org to purchase your patch.

• • •

Teach a child to swim. Swimming is great exercise,
and so fun! Spend time getting your kids, nieces,
nephews, or neighborhood kids more comfortable
in the water. Your gesture of *kindness* will
provide a skill that lasts a lifetime!

Volunteer to be a leader in a children's hiking or scouting group. Not only will you be working with young people, teaching important skills in a fun way, but you will also be serving as an example of a volunteer who believes in the power of *kindness*.

Rally against genetically modified organisms (GMOs). Safe food should not be a privilege. Find out how you can *join the fight* against GMOs by visiting Fight Against GMOs (www.fightagainstgmos.com).

●●●

Buy a goat for a family in a developing country. This small *gesture* will help the family in myriad ways. The family will have goat's milk to drink and will be able to sell the extra. Goat manure will enrich the soil enabling the family to grow a crop, which can be sold for money. Visit World Vision (https://donate.worldvision .org/ways-to-give) to find out more.

●●●

Promote the *preservation* of women's art. Support female cultural heritage by backing art, music, literature, and dance. The more you support these endeavors, the more chances a young girl has at attaining her artistic dreams.

Be a *mentor* to one or more students.
No matter their age, they could benefit greatly from
having an older, responsible person guiding them.
This may be especially true of children living in
single-parent households.

●●○

Show Mother Earth some *kindness* this Earth Day.
April 22 is when the world's attention is focused on
making our planet a healthier place for all to live.
Organize a cleanup in conjunction with the holiday. Visit
the day's official website—www.earthday.org—so you
can coordinate your efforts with others across the globe.

●●○

Lend your signature to a cause at Care2.
This organization has joined in partnership with the
Wildlife Conservation Society and also the Nature
Conservancy to do *good* for environmental causes. Visit
www.care2.com to see how you can join or start a petition.

End the needless suffering of animals. Become a member of the Animal Welfare Institute. Your membership fee will *help* the organization stop a number of unnecessary acts of animal cruelty. Sign up today at www.awionline.org.

● ● ●

Make your shopping *count*. Rather than just acquiring stuff, shop and give to charity at the same time. Purchase items in the Hunger Site, Literacy Site, Rainforest Site, and Animal Rescue Site stores at the GreaterGood website. See www.greatergood.com for more information.

● ● ●

Sponsor a woman in need. Women for Women International (www.womenforwomen .org) helps women in war-ravaged countries such as Afghanistan and Rwanda to rebuild their lives. Visit the site to learn about sponsorship and volunteering. You can also send a message of *support* or shop the bazaar.

Recycle your coffee grounds. Keep an empty coffee can in your kitchen to collect the grounds after brewing. You can either deposit them in your compost or fertilize your garden.

• • •

Donate your books and DVDs to a local library. The library can sell them during a fundraising event to generate funds to purchase new library materials or equipment.

• • •

Babysit for a single parent or family in need for free. Childcare costs can be a burden and can stop a single parent or family from earning their much-needed maximum potential income. If you can offer to help for a couple of hours here and there, your act of *kindness* and generosity can make a difference.

Donate your tools.
Help a village *lift* itself out
of poverty through micro-
enterprise. Check out www
.sustainablevillage.com
and see how you can help
them succeed.

Control pests *naturally*. Take a class on how to control pests in your yard and garden using natural means and companion plantings rather than using products that poison or otherwise harm the earth. Find information on sustainable crops, use of manure, and companion planting at www.attra.org/attra-pub/complant.html.

●●●

Become a conservation volunteer. Work with the parks and recreation department to *restore* natural habitats while learning about ecology, botany, local wildlife, and public land management issues. Build a path, plant trees and bushes, or do something else that is good for preserving or creating green spaces in your community.

●●●

Start an oral history project about your community. Get students to interview senior citizens. A collection of their personal histories and *memories* of the community and world can be housed in a local library or public center.

Protect endangered species of birds.
Do something to *help* ensure that the whooping crane, the Mexican spotted owl, the ivory-billed woodpecker, and the Puerto Rican parrot, along with hundreds of other birds, do not go extinct. Find out more at www.audubon.org/birds/priority.

• • •

Plan a holiday party for your neighbors. Initiate setting up the logistics on your street. Get at least two other neighbors to help you. Plan a traveling dinner: appetizers at one house, salad and soup at the next, the entrée at the third house, and desserts at the fourth. Spread the spirit of *kindness* this holiday season!

Call an elderly relative
just to say hello.
Your *kindness* will
brighten his or her day.

Sponsor an acre of rain forest.
Make a $40 *donation* in the name of
someone for whom you would otherwise
purchase a birthday gift or anniversary
present. See www.rainforestconcern.org.

●●●

Teach a budding *artist* a new craft.
Show her how to knit a sweater, mold clay on
a potter's wheel, hammer together a birdhouse,
crochet a blanket, etch a piece of glass, embroider
a pillowcase, apply mosaic to a ceramic picture
frame, or sew a traditional quilt.

●●●

Make a donation to your local parks department.
Parks and public places are for all to *share*—your
contribution will help them to become better places
for everyone in your community to enjoy.

Help a child with a math problem. Encourage and direct her toward the solution, but don't give her the answer. Use coins or blocks to help her understand the problem. Allow her to *discover* the solution on her own.

●●●

Motivate a friend. Everyone needs a little push now and then to do something. Perhaps she wants to lose weight or learn how to deep-sea dive, dance the Argentine tango, cook a chocolate soufflé, or speak Greek. Gently and *kindly* urge her to go for it! You might even want to join in. It'll do you both some good.

●●●

Recycle using Freecycle.org. If there isn't one where you live, start a Freecycle branch. The Freecycle Network is a virtual organization of and for people who wish to recycle rather than throw stuff into landfills. Find items you *need* and get them free or post items that you want to give away at www.freecycle.org.

Take a volunteer vacation. Want to travel but don't want to fight through crowds of tourists or lie idle on a beach? Consider taking a volunteer vacation where you can do *good* while seeing new sights. Organizations such as Global Volunteers (www.globalvolunteers.org) and International Volunteer Programs Association (www .volunteerinternational.org) can help you plan your trip.

●●●

Adopt a section of a highway.
Organize a group to help you pick up trash
along your designated section of the road.
It goes a long way toward keeping our
environment *beautiful*.

●●●

Volunteer with the National Children's Coalition.
This organization *helps* at-risk kids who are runaways,
abused, or suffer from addiction. Help where others
have given up. For more information see
www.teenzeen.org/volunteer.html.

Donate an old car to charity. Give your old car *new* life in the hands of a new owner who can use it for their charity, or sell parts for cash. Many charities accept automobile donations, so do online research to find where your wheels will best be put to use.

●●●

Give a clean glass of water. The money from giving up a cup of gourmet latte every day for one week could buy a micro filter to ensure a developing nation's school drinking water was *safe*. Visit www.unicefusa.org to donate toward the safe drinking water cause.

●●●

Teach a child how to tie her shoelaces. Demonstrate how to tie the laces with one shoe and let her *practice* on her other shoe.

●●●

Build your vocabulary and end hunger— at the same time. Visit www.freerice.com and play a simple (but addictive) vocabulary game. For every word you get right, the organization *donates* twenty grains of rice through the UN's World Food Programme.

Walk your neighbor's dog. If your neighbor doesn't have time to join you on your walk, offer to take his pet for a brisk walk. *Enjoy* the day and the sights of the neighborhoods.

Donate to the Elephant Sanctuary.
Elephants come from all over the world to *rest* at this
sanctuary. By visiting the website at www.elephants.com
you can even watch them on the live webcam!

● ● ●

Do your part to *clean* the shores.
Join the worldwide effort to clean up
trash lying along the shorelines of the
world's oceans, rivers, and lakes. For more
information see www.oceanconservancy.org.

● ● ●

Plant bulbs around your house. With the help of your
family, plant them in front of your house, next to the ugly
parking strip in front, or along the front entrance walkway.
Your neighbors will be looking out their windows to
enjoy the flowers you planted and will appreciate you
taking the time and effort to create such a display.

Send a postcard to a child in your life.
Next time you travel, jot off a quick hello and
let him know about the place you're visiting.
Write a simple message crafted for his reading
level. Include drawings or stickers. Children
love getting mail addressed to them.

● ● ●

Empower women around the world. Make a donation
to the Women's Learning Partnership. This organization
helps women in developing countries network and
gain the leadership skills they need to *transform*
themselves, their families, and their societies. Visit
www.learningpartnership.org to see how you can help.

● ● ●

Defend the earth. Become a member of the Natural
Resources Defense Council (NRDC) and join the effort
to fight to *save* the nation's wildlife and wild places.
Check out the NRDC website at www.nrdc.org.

Support local farms. Local and family farms are quickly becoming a thing of the past. *Support* them by buying locally grown produce and by donating to Farm Aid (www.farmaid.org).

Plant a tree. Urban forests help improve air quality. Trees absorb carbon dioxide and release oxygen into the atmosphere. One tree gives enough oxygen back through photosynthesis to support two human beings. To discover other interesting facts about trees, go to http://coloradotrees.org; to plant a tree *in memory* of a loved one, visit www.arborday.org.

•••

Create an arts program for underprivileged children. Form a group *committed* to teaching about the arts and reach out to your community. Maybe your strength lies in the area of finance, public relations, art education, or networking. Whatever it is, use your expertise to help develop and launch the program.

•••

Be *kind* to the earth by recycling old Christmas cards. Cut out pieces and use them as gift tags. Or turn them into new cards or collage materials for kids.

If your city or town does not have a recycling program, make it happen. Get *support* from other eco-conscious citizens and petition your local politicians.

• • •

Set a good example. Be respectful toward others and exhibit *kindness* at all times. When you say "yes, Ma'am," and "yes, Sir," you are showing respect. Don't forget to say "please" and "thank you." Young people used to learn proper etiquette and manners in finishing schools. Now it is up to parents to teach youngsters how to conduct themselves in social situations.

• • •

Make a contribution to the World Health Organization (WHO). This is a branch of the United Nations that works to ensure good health for all humanity. Every minute a mother dies in childbirth. The WHO has a program on maternal, newborn, child, and adolescent *health*. Check out www.who.int/maternal_child_adolescent/en/.

Stop the proliferation of guns. If you are concerned about the role of weapons in domestic violence, school killings, and armed conflict in the world, join *efforts* toward tougher arms controls. Visit www.controlarms.org to see what you can do to stop gun violence.

● ● ●

Protest injustice wherever and whenever you see it. Get *involved* in stopping it. If you believe that all humans possess a disposition toward compassion and a sense of the interconnectedness of us all, then fight for equal justice for everyone.

● ● ●

Volunteer your language services online. Do some *good* for the world using your writing or translating skills. Bilingual people are needed for translation work and other cyberspace tasks. Go to www.onlinevolunteering.org to sign up.

Sign up to be a bone marrow donor.
This decision could help *save* someone else's life.
On an average day, doctors search the database in order
to match six thousand men, women, and children with
potential donors. Learn how you can be a part of this
donor database at https://bethematch.org.

● ● ●

Help volunteers volunteer.
Make a donation to VolunteerMatch
(www.volunteermatch.org), which helps
people find the *perfect* place to volunteer
their time and do their own good.

● ● ●

Use sand instead of corrosive salt. Keep two milk
cartons filled with sand in the trunk of your car.
Next time your tires are spinning on snow or ice,
pour the sand under them for *traction*.

Check in regularly on
elderly relatives or
neighbors. In extreme
heat or cold, pop in to
see if they need anything.
And even when the
weather is mild, stop in
to share a cup of tea and
conversation. A little touch
of *kindness* can go
a long way!

Leave your estate to a preservation organization. Groups such as the Conservation Foundation (www.the conservationfoundation.org) accept estates for land and watershed preservation. Land endowments preserve natural resources and ensure that future generations will have *beautiful* places on the earth to enjoy.

• • •

Fight hate with *kindness*. Help the Southern Poverty Law Center teach tolerance and seek justice for victims of hate crimes. To learn how you can help and become involved in the movement go to www.splcenter.org.

• • •

Shovel the snow from your neighbor's steps. Shoveling snow can be a very arduous task. Help out your neighbors who might need an extra hand. *Offer* to shovel their steps, driveway, and walkway, and take only their "thank you" as compensation.

Save the polar bear. Considered the world's largest terrestrial carnivore, the polar bear is in danger of becoming extinct by the end of this century because of climate changes affecting its frozen habitat. Learn more at www.worldwildlife.org/polarbears.

• • •

Unplug electrical items not in use. Some cell phone chargers, for example, continue to use electrical current even after a cell phone has been removed from it.

• • •

Choose the fish you eat *carefully*. Some fish populations have been depleted due to overfishing. Check out www.goodfishguide.org and click on "Fish to avoid" to learn more.

• • •

Go *batty*. Buy a bat house, adopt a bat, or make a donation to Bat Conservation International. Bats devour garden pests and their guano is a natural fertilizer. To make a donation visit www.batcon.org.

Collect *toys* for
children living in
homeless shelters.

Help stop child hunger. Children living in third-world countries do not get enough to eat and go without clean drinking water. Create *good karma* by making a little sacrifice in your lifetime to ensure that a child does not have to endure hunger for another day. Donate a week's worth of money you would spend on going out to eat to www.feedthechildren.org.

●●●

Propagate and share your plants. Give out plants and flowers that yours spawn to local groups and neighbors interested in *beautifying* your neighborhood or community. You will enjoy seeing your plants throughout your community.

●●●

Spend time doing puzzles and playing card games. Gather the family *together* for an afternoon of unplugged fun. The emphasis is on the quality of time spent together, not the cost of the entertainment.

Use handkerchiefs instead of tissues. It cuts down on paper waste. Find *pretty* handkerchiefs at thrift stores and secondhand shops or make them from white cotton, cut into squares and hemmed. Decorate with embroidery or stamped art.

●●●

Help a young family off the plane. Parents traveling with small children have plenty to carry—babies, diaper bags, toys, and a stroller. They were allowed to board first, but the same is not true for when the plane lands and they have to disembark. If you are seated near them, do what you can to *help* them get off.

●●●

Give your old sewing machine to a local school. When you are ready to buy a newer model, donate your old machine. A *student* in an art or fashion design program without the means to afford a machine might be able to use it.

Help a war orphan. Visit www.warchild.org and learn about the atrocities millions of children face daily as they confront the horrors of war. Make a donation to the organization on its website and help make a *difference* in these children's lives.

● ● ●

Return programs before leaving exhibits. When leaving a cultural event or museum, tuck the catalog back into its slot for others to use rather than taking it home to toss into the recycling bin.

● ● ●

Deliver some homemade lemonade. When a friend receives some bad news, take a pitcher and two glasses to her house, sit down with her, and enjoy a glass together. Sip and be silent while she talks or cries. You are with her to show *love* and support.

Let your employees know they're *appreciated*. Make sure your workers know they are wanted with congratulatory emails when they achieve their goals or just a verbal acknowledgment when they've had a great week. People are less likely to switch jobs if they feel they are making a contribution that is appreciated.

● ● ●

Organize an open studios event. If you are an art lover and know struggling artists in your community, arrange for other art enthusiasts to visit the studios or homes of local artists and purchase artwork. Everyone *benefits*.

● ● ●

Reduce CO_2 emissions. With global warming such a hot topic these days it's *easy* to learn ways to decrease the size of your carbon footprint. Start small like bringing reusable bags with you to the grocery store. Making changes little by little will make a large impact on the health of the environment. For more tips visit http://planetark.org.

Leave anonymous
May Day flowers. Every
May 1 is May Day, and
tradition dictates that you
leave someone flowers to
brighten up her day.
This is a great way to
make someone smile.

Donate to the World Wildlife Federation. When you give money to this *all-important* cause you'll be helping endangered species worldwide. With more and more species being added to the endangered list every year, the animals need your help now more than ever. Visit www.wwf.org for more information.

● ● ●

Open up your home. Offer an empty room to a university student looking to live off campus. It will help him or her financially, and you can forge a *friendship* with a young person just setting out in the world.

● ● ●

Buy chickens for a family. Instead of donating cash, why not donate an animal or two? A family can enjoy—and share—the eggs from the chickens that they raise. Part of Heifer International's mission is to have the family pass along the offspring from their animals, creating a *community* of giving (www.heifer.org).

Donate to keep the planet *diverse*.
Support the work of the International Union for Conservation of Nature (IUCN). The organization strives to conserve and preserve the earth's diversity of nature. See www.iucn.org.

●●●

Consider making your house solar; you'll save money on electricity and do the earth a *favor*. Visit Google's Project Sunroof at www.google.com/get/sunroof for more information.

●●●

When you return from vacation, give street maps, foreign coins, subway tickets, and extra postcards to a child. These "treasures" make *great* items for Show and Tell!

●●●

Join the monumental endeavor to help scientists predict climate change. It is just one way *shared* computing power is working. For more information see www.climateprediction.net.

Leave an encouraging note. If you notice someone in your office is having a particularly bad day, stick a Post-it on her desk with an encouraging message. She will appreciate the *kind* words.

Help *protect* the whales. Though whaling is illegal,
it is still common practice in some areas of the world.
Organizations like the Sea Shepherd Conservation Society
are working to shut down this inhumane practice. For
more information visit www.seashepherd.org.

●●●

Make a loan to entrepreneurs across the globe to help
them create better lives for themselves and their families.
Kiva (www.kiva.org) works with microfinance institutions
on five continents to provide loans to people without
access to traditional banking systems. For as little
as $25 you can help give someone an opportunity to
transform their business and their life.

●●●

Grab a friend and learn to dance.
It's good for your *heart* and your friend's too.
You both get a healthy workout and have some
fun. Better still, you are supporting each
other's goals of staying healthy.

Pamper your pooch. Give him homemade, dog-healthy biscuits. These extra-effort treats will show your pet how much you *care*—and are healthier alternatives to the processed variety. Find a recipe at www.gourmetsleuth.com.

●●●

Get children out of the fields. *Stop* the forced labor of children in the agriculture industries of the world. According to Human Rights Watch, more than 69 percent of the 218 million children doing child labor are working in agriculture. See http://hrw.org/children/labor.htm.

●●●

Invite the new hire out to lunch. Starting a new job is hard. Help the new person in your office and invite him out to lunch. A little *kindness* goes a long way!

Make it a point to *remember* people's names.
People who remember names are often deemed
respectful and caring. Associate a colleague's name with
one of his or her physical features to help you remember.

● ● ●

Return elderly neighbors' empty garbage cans.
Going outside in inclement weather requires special
effort and elderly people risk a dangerous fall. Your
act of *kindness* eliminates that risk.

● ● ●

Adopt an endangered species. Organizations
are making it fun to donate by letting you adopt an
endangered species; often they'll tell you fun facts about
your species like where their habitat is and how your
donation will help to keep them off of the endangered list.

● ● ●

Send a child to music camp. If you know of a child who
loves music but can't afford an instrument or can't
afford to go to camp, help any way you can.

Hold a yard sale and donate the proceeds to a charity. You'll get rid of your junk and make a difference in the world at the same time. People are less likely to haggle if they know that their money is *supporting* a worthy cause!

● ● ●

Help a neighbor with a home improvement project. You can *steady* a ladder, hand him a tool, or hold something in place.

● ● ●

Watch a pet while its owner's on vacation. Take the responsibility seriously and *care* for the animal exactly as you are instructed. Make certain you have phone numbers and know how to deal with emergencies that may arise.

● ● ●

Help a coworker succeed. By helping others get ahead, you increase your chances for success as well. Besides it's good karma for you. We all need a champion in our corner. Be a *champion* for someone else. When you climb up the career ladder, pull someone up behind you.

Plan a nature hike with your children. Point out *pretty* stones, wildlife, flowers, and other things along the way. Children love such walks and will especially enjoy it because you are with them.

Give fair trade presents. Next time you need a birthday, holiday, or "just because" present, skip the obvious and head for a store where you'll find *unique* items that also do good internationally. At stores like Ten Thousand Villages (www.tenthousandvillages.com) and Serrv (www.serrv.org) you'll find lots of fair trade goodies that will make the perfect gift.

● ● ●

Donate a wheelchair to someone in a developing country. Through the Free Wheelchair Mission (www.freewheelchairmission.org) you can *provide* a wheelchair to someone in need.

● ● ●

Make a contribution to an entrepreneur. If you want to make a donation and know that it's making a very *specific* difference, look into an organization like the Foundation for International Community Assistance (FINCA, at www.finca.org). These companies allow you to make a loan to an entrepreneur in the developing world and learn the specific use of the money.

Share your home office equipment. Allow a friend to use your computer, printer, or scanner. It's likely your equipment isn't in use all day, and giving your friend *access* will save him the time and expense of going to a copy center.

● ● ●

Empower people to make change in their community. Take *inspiration* from Medical Ambassadors International, an organization that works in rural villages to help local leaders address their community's problems of poverty and disease by looking at the root causes. For information visit www.medicalambassadors.org.

● ● ●

Set up a fundraising website. You don't need to be doing a specific event to have a fundraising website. Check out the site started by Kevin Bacon, www.sixdegrees.org, for more information. On this site you can compete with other charities to see who can *raise* the most funds.

Perform music for
retirement home residents.
The center's residents will
love it, and you'll feel good
about *sharing* your
talent to lighten the heart
of someone else.

Attend a rally for a good cause. It's hard to ignore thousands of people all gathered *together* for the same cause. Even if you can't make it to the nation's capital to voice your opinion, rallies are held nationally. Can't find one for your cause? Start one yourself by hanging fliers and posting online.

● ● ●

Recycle nonrecyclable materials. Companies like TerraCycle (www.terracycle.net) are taking packaging materials from products like energy bars and drink pouches and making them into *new products*, from tote bags to homework folders. You can mail in your used materials or drop them off at a local center.

● ● ●

Organize a neighborhood beautification project. Try to get everyone involved. Whether it is decorating for the holidays or planting a rose bush in every yard for a garden party, the point is to get everyone *involved* in meeting each other and working together for the greater good of the neighborhood.

Get in shape for a good cause. Earn money for medical research teams and exercise at the same time by participating in a charity walk. There are many to choose from, so seek out a walk associated with a cause you feel *passionate* about.

● ● ●

Report on local businesses' greenness. Websites are popping up where you can rate how green a business is and *recommend* an eco-friendly business to others. Check out www.izzitgreen.com for more information.

● ● ●

Stop using pesticides. These chemical treatments can harm the planet and run off into water supplies. Find organic *solutions* to deter crop infestation, such as companion planting. Use damp newspapers placed on the ground at night in the garden to attract slugs. The next morning, throw away the papers.

Organize a day of silence.
The Day of Silence initiative was started
to end harassment of LGBT youth, but the style
of action can be used to draw *attention*
to other causes as well.

●●●

Contribute to a first response backpack.
The packs are distributed to soldiers wounded on
the battlefield. There are no longer MASH units to
offer military medical assistance in the arena of combat.
The wounded are transported to military hospitals,
often without so much as a toothbrush or change
of clothes. The backpack contains personal items.
See www.operationfirstresponse.org/ofr-backpacks
for more information.

●●●

Let go of the need to hold on to the past.
You cannot undo what has been done. It's history.
Embrace the present and dream of tomorrow.

Embrace your family members' lifestyle choices. *Respect* the rights of your loved ones to follow the paths that you may not agree with but that they have chosen. Keep your mouth shut, don't judge them—just remain firm in your support and love.

●●●

Offer financial support for refugees. Migrants often seek asylum for reasons of persecution or poverty. If life becomes untenable in their native land, they are forced to move. Often rape, torture, and the lack of economic sources to sustain them leaves them traumatized and destitute. Donate to the cause at www.amnestyusa.org.

●●●

Reduce the noise in your office. Cut down on yelling or talking loudly, playing music too loudly, or creating a commotion as you walk down the hallway. Studies indicate that problem-solving will *improve* and stress will go down. So do yourself and your coworkers a favor and reduce the noise to improve your productivity.

Help unload a neighbor's car. If you see a neighbor unloading his or her bags from the car after a shopping trip, *offer* to help take the bags inside.

Be mindful of your souvenirs.
Travel to other lands to learn about other cultures but be *respectful* to the local people and honorable in your dealings. Do not purchase items such as cultural treasures (where removal is prohibited), banned resources, or extinct or endangered species.

● ● ●

Play matchmaker. Have a party and invite two people you know would hit it off. *Introduce* them at the party and see what happens. Who knows...they may spend the rest of their married life thanking you.

● ● ●

Call out litter bugs. Voice your exasperation when you see someone littering on our public paths, streets, or highways. Remind the individual that the planet belongs to all of us and we all share a *responsibility* to keep it clean. Also, litter is a misdemeanor offense in most communities that is punishable by a fine.

Become a human rights *activist*. Let your government know that you do not want terrorism to be the excuse used to violate human rights—yours or anyone else's. Go to www.amnestyusa.org and pledge your support.

● ● ●

Become more *accepting* of your colleagues. People have different work habits, skills, and abilities. Accept coworkers for the talents and skills that they have.

● ● ●

Bring a game to your grandparent's retirement home. Meet regularly with your grandparent and others to play bridge, poker, mahjong, or bingo. The point is to reach out to the one you love and bring people *together*.

● ● ●

Provide a child with the *confidence* to do new things. Children who are encouraged to try their best and then succeed develop great self-confidence.

Prepare a hot drink for your mailperson in the cold weather. Ready a cup of cocoa, tea, or coffee and have it waiting for the letter carrier out delivering mail on a cold and snowy day.

Make your next dinner or cocktail gathering a party with a *purpose*. Put out decorative boxes for donations and theme the event around the charity that you're collecting for. For help choosing a worthy organization to donate to visit www.charitywatch.org or www.charitynavigator.org.

●●●

Shop sweatshop-free. If you take a moment to research where your clothing comes from, you may be inspired to shop sweatshop-free. Organizations like No Sweat Apparel (www.nosweatapparel.com) are working to rid the world of sweatshops and *promote* a living wage for workers, one item of clothing at a time.

●●●

Boycott intolerant companies. Along with *like-minded* friends, refuse to support or give money to any organization, network, or company that practices bigotry, racism, or any other morally indefensible behavior.

Write a letter. There are ways to help that take as little effort as picking up a pen. By writing a letter to your congressperson you can let him or her know that you are *counting* on him or her to help make a difference internationally. Many organizations even have sample letters you can use on their website. All you need to do is find the address of your local representative and mail it in.

●●●

Send *books* to Africa.
Through the organization Books for Africa (www.booksforafrica.org), you can donate books to be sent to countries in Africa.

●●●

Become a volunteer teacher abroad. Similar to their medical counterpart, Teachers Without Borders sends volunteer teachers to countries that are lacking proper education. They also *provide* professional development for teachers worldwide. To sign up or sponsor a teacher visit www.teacherswithoutborders.org.

Chaperone an outing at your teenager's school.
Whether it's a ski trip or a weekend camping,
be *involved* in your teen's life.

• • •

Help others in need on Halloween by encouraging
the children in your life to *participate* in Trick-
or-Treat for UNICEF each year. Not to worry: they can
still get candy while trick-or-treating, but this way they're
also helping to make a difference in the world. UNICEF
is a United Nations organization that helps children
worldwide. Visit www.unicefusa.org/trick-or-treat
for more information and to order the Trick-or-
Treat for UNICEF boxes.

• • •

Be *mindful* of the little things.
Tell a neighbor if you see a car parked
with the lights left on or a trunk or door open.
You could save your neighbor time
and money in the long run.

Keep in touch with family who live far away.
Write often, call when you can, and send a
holiday card with photos. Fill the card with words of
kindness and good cheer.

● ● ●

Make a donation to Asha for Education—
and get your company to match your contribution.
With your *support*, this organization helps to
provide an education to underprivileged children in
India. Visit its website (www.ashanet.org) for more
information and to make your donation.

● ● ●

Partner with the United Nations to address
sustainable development. Join a project or create
your own; check out the UN-Business Action Hub at
https://business.un.org and sign up today.

Bring in a box
of doughnuts for
everyone
in the office.

Volunteer with Habitat for Humanity. This and similar organizations build houses to shelter *humankind*. In order to rid the world of poverty housing and homelessness, Habitat for Humanity seeks dedicated volunteers to assist in the effort. Find information at www.habitat.org.

● ● ●

Save a quarter a day. While it might be hard to budget donating large lump sums to organizations, consider setting aside a quarter a day in a hunger fund. Once the quarters start to pile up, take them to the bank and then write out a check (see www.bread.org for donating to hunger organizations).

● ● ●

Clean a friend's garage. Take your broom, dustpan, and some garbage bags to a friend or neighbor's house and help him *clean* out his garage.

Become an animal advocate. Join the network of animal advocates working within the Humane Action Network, a grassroots organization seeking legal *protections* for animals against cruel treatment and suffering. See www.humanesociety.org for more information.

● ● ●

Be *courteous* in foreign airports and hotels. Download a foreign language phrase app and make an attempt to ask for what you need in the language of the country you are in. Most airport personnel are happy to help you, and you may discover that the individual helping you speaks English, but don't assume it.

● ● ●

Encourage others to *support* local businesses. Spread the word to your neighbors about local businesses you have had good experiences with—help support them by word-of-mouth marketing.

Offer to help in your local library's children's section. Children who *love* stories are more likely to develop a love for books—and good reading skills help children perform better in school.

Send an impromptu thank-you email. If a business associate goes out of her way for you, tell her how much you appreciate her unexpected *kindness*. While expressing your gratitude, mention how much your association with her means to you.

● ● ●

Cook for your dog. Research natural dog food recipes online. With your vet's blessing, a diet adjustment may *improve* health and cut down on his ingestion of artificial ingredients.

● ● ●

Help vaccinate the poor. Join forces with Shared, Inc., a nonprofit, tax-exempt organization that works to increase the *availability* of vaccines and vital medicines to the world's poorest individuals. Shared aligns with other partners and individuals to accomplish its goals. For information go to www.healthshares.org.

● ● ●

Adopt a soldier. Make a commitment to send a care package to your soldier one to two times a month. To start an adoption see www.soldiersangels.org.

Support the work of international journalists who are monitoring the issues of press freedom, working to reduce censorship, trying to *safeguard* journalists (especially in war zones), publishing reports about press freedom, defending journalists, and protesting the imprisonment of journalists such as those considered cyber dissidents by the Chinese government for writing on the Internet. For more information see www.rsf.org/en.

● ● ●

Stand in your spouse's shoes. Before you give in to the urge to let go a barrage of accusations and complaints against your life partner and lover, why not try to stand for a while in his shoes to get *perspective*.

● ● ●

Help rid the world of landmines. Raise money with friends by hosting a dinner party and charging an attendance fee. Donate the money to ban landmines. Children are often the victims. Roughly $100 can *help* a child with an amputated leg walk again. See www.icbl.org.

Let your *elected officials* know that you are against your government conducting torture of POWs in violation of Article 5 of the Universal Declaration of Human Rights (1948) that states, "No one shall be subjected to torture or to cruel, inhuman or degrading treatment or punishment."

● ● ●

Support Food Not Bombs. Food Not Bombs is an organization that *actively* protests war and shares vegetarian food with the hungry at the same time. To donate food or money, or to learn more, visit www.foodnotbombs.net.

● ● ●

Help end global poverty. Make a donation to Make Poverty History. The organization offers a white wristband to raise *awareness* for the cause. Visit www.makepovertyhistory.org to pledge your support.

Become an employee of the United Nations.
Be a professional policy advisor or worker in another specialized field of the UN. There are many different needs for more than 140 countries. There are a *variety* of jobs to be done requiring diverse skills. Such jobs include crisis prevention specialists to policy advisors, microcredit specialists, and educators. See https://careers.un.org.

●●●

Prepare the next generation to keep the *peace*. Donate or volunteer with Seeds of Peace (www.seedsofpeace.org) and help develop the next generation of peacemakers.

●●●

Gather up your old eyeglasses and donate them to Unite for Sight at www.uniteforsight.org. People toss out millions of pairs of eyeglasses each year—*eyewear* that could benefit people with vision loss in the developing world.

Hug a girlfriend after her breakup. Honor her emotions, *empathize* with her pain, but resist telling her about your own breakups, offering platitudes, or giving advice. If she needs to talk, listen. If she needs to cry, give her tissues and hugs.

Lobby for living wage jobs worldwide. Join efforts of others to call global governments into action and *create* living wage jobs for everyone. Simply making sure everyone is fairly compensated for his or her work will cut down on worldwide poverty.

• • •

Link up with other like-minded people.
Make an effort to meet other politically active people by attending political rallies, working with charitable fundraisers, and joining environmental groups for hikes, bird watching, or biking trips. When you join communities of like-minded people, you have more *power* to effect change, get laws enacted, and do good works.

• • •

Help fight disease *globally* with Doctors Without Borders (www.doctorswithoutborders.org). This organization provides much more than just vaccinations and medical care to communities that don't have the means to do so themselves. Visit their website to set up a monthly donation.

Volunteer with Water for People.
Dirty water is one of the leading causes of sickness
in underdeveloped communities. Join the *fight* for
clean water at www.waterforpeople.org.

● ● ●

Participate in a Relay for Life. Sponsored by the
American Cancer Society, these overnight events
are held in cities and towns across the country.
Learn how you can form a *team* and participate
in a relay in your area at www.relayforlife.org.

● ● ●

Advocate World AIDS Day. December 1 is World AIDS
Day. Host an event to raise *awareness* about the
global impact of AIDS. Hand out a list of organizations
that help people suffering from AIDS worldwide so that
people can choose to donate. Include organizations that
specifically help women, orphans displaced by AIDS,
or are working on a cure; that way people can put their
money where they feel the most passionately.

Make a donation in

your friend's name to

his or her

favorite charity.

Be a pen pal to someone in the armed services.
No one wants to feel alone and forgotten. This is a way to help a soldier serving in a foreign land know he has a *friend*. Visit www.soldiersangels.org/letter-writing-team.html to learn how you can join.

●●●

Take a *stand* against genocide.
Educate yourself about how it happens and what can be done to stop it. Even after the horrors of the Nazi Holocaust, genocide has occurred in Darfur, Rwanda, Sudan, Iraq, and elsewhere. Check out www.genocidewatch .com to see how you can help.

●●●

Start your family's day with an *inspiring* quote.
It will replay in their minds throughout the day and reenergize them toward their goals. Write it on a piece of paper and stick it on the fridge, tape it to the back door, or slip a copy into everyone's pocket—in short, make it accessible to read throughout the day.

Encourage countries to "think outside the bomb." Several countries have declared themselves nuclear weapons–free zones. *Encourage* other countries to do the same by visiting www.icanw.org.

● ● ●

Help provide medical supplies to those in need. By volunteering with MedShare (www.medshare.org) you can make sure that hospitals in developing areas of the world have the *necessary* medical equipment.

● ● ●

Volunteer to mentor young entrepreneurs. If you have business expertise that you could *share* with others, contact your local community small business organization to lend your support to entrepreneurs and owners of start-up companies.

● ● ●

Repair reused items. Head to an architectural salvage yard before the hardware store to find fixtures, flooring, banisters, and hardware supplies.

Buy *fresh* eggs from a local farm. This will help both the farm and you. Your purchase will be put to good use, helping with the daily maintenance and possible expansion of the farm. And the fresh eggs will taste better in your omelets, salads, and cakes.

● ● ●

Take off your shoes at the door. Wearing slippers or socks indoors instead of shoes will *prolong* the time between the eco-damaging and expensive cleaning of carpets.

● ● ●

Give away gardening supplies. Rather than throwing away the things you don't use anymore, choose to pass them on to other gardeners. Put potted plants, old firewood, unwanted gardening tools, bags of bulbs, and extra garden pots on the curb in front of your apartment or house with a sign that states: Free for the Taking.

Use environmentally *friendly* household cleaners. Many household cleaners on the market leave toxins in your environment (which in this case is your house!). Make the smart decision and use all-natural cleaning products.

• • •

Become a part of your town's disaster relief team. When a natural disaster has hit or is about to hit your hometown, you can help out. Whether it's building sandbag walls or volunteering at evacuation centers, you can play an *important* role in everyone else's safety.

• • •

Endow a scholarship at a local school. Start a scholarship program for local high school students looking to go to college. As tuition prices keep increasing, the next generation of students will need all the help they can get. You will need to contribute a significant amount of money for the principal endowment—the awards are then gifted from the principal's earnings—but it's worth it.

Give away your old dishware, pans, and utensils. Think of a family who may not have many household items or money to buy what they need. Your *kindness* will go a long way.

Teach an aged relative how to do seated stretching. These *exercises* will help him remain limber and keep his muscles toned. Put on music that he likes and make it a pleasurable experience for you both.

● ● ●

Spend time with a child who has an absent family member. Your *companionship* will help fill the void suffered by the child. Commit to that child and his family to be another stable and secure person in his life.

● ● ●

Resist killing a helpful pest. Escort a honeybee, mosquito eater, or spider out the door rather than squashing it. The bee pollinates the garden, while the spider and mosquito eater consume pests and are *beneficial* to your plants.

● ● ●

Instead of purchasing your milk in plastic or cardboard containers, opt for glass. These can be *recycled* or reused.

Hold a fundraiser to support a hospital. Organize family members of people who have received or are about to have an organ transplant. *Together* plan a holiday boutique to sell donated and handmade items such as quilts, painted cookie tins, ornaments, and holiday napkin rings and table linens. Set up in the hospital lobby and donate the money to a hospital department that needs funds to buy equipment or care for a family without resources to stay near a loved one undergoing a transplant.

●●●

Volunteer at an animal *rescue* facility. You could do something as simple as answering the phones.

●●●

Donate your old cell phones to *charity*. It's estimated that more than 150 million cell phones are lying around in office desk drawers and in homes. Check out www.phones4charity.com. Phones 4 Charity takes phones that work as well as broken ones, recycling the latter in accordance with federal and local environmental standards.

Give away your extra blankets. Look around your house for spare blankets and linens, wash them, and donate them to a community shelter for the homeless. Your *kindness* will warm body and soul!

Donate your old magazines to a school. Clean the clutter of magazines from around your house and donate those to a local school. Even if they are old, they can be used for *art projects*.

●●●

Try a different type of tree this Christmas. Instead of supporting an industry that chops down pine or fir trees each year to use as Christmas trees, consider a *potted* herb, such as rosemary sheared in the shape of a holiday tree. Planted in a container, it will continue to grow.

●●●

Support an environmental cause.
Figure out what you're really passionate about (water conservation, land preservation, recycling, etc.) and make a commitment of time, energy, and creative input. It might be elections of a local school board or a city issue of where to put a new parking lot that affects the local environment. Decide where you stand and then get *involved* and do some good.

Opt for energy-*efficient* steel-belted radial tires. If inflated properly and regularly rotated, such tires can last over 100,000 miles. This will help cut down on rubber waste caused by disposal of old tires.

● ● ●

Give a child a job during his school break. The child could paint your fence, clear rocks from your garden, or wash windows. The point is to give a child something *meaningful* to do that enables him to earn money.

● ● ●

Read to the blind. You can record audio versions of newspapers, books, and magazines for the visually impaired. Check out Learning Ally (www.learningally.org).

● ● ●

Participate in a disaster *cleanup* effort. Volunteer to help clean up debris after a tornado, earthquake, hurricane, flood, wildfire, or other natural disaster.

Pick up trash. If you see litter, don't just let it bother you; get out there and pick it up! Be inspired by Robin Kevan, known as "Rob the Rubbish," whose disdain for litter led him to clean up the streets of his small Welsh town. Following that successful campaign, Rob went on to *clean up* trails on peaks in Scotland and Wales, and even Mount Everest.

• • •

Set up a fundraiser for school supplies. As schools struggle financially to pay for teachers, facilities, and supplies, parents are increasingly being asked to help out with classroom expenses. The *education* of our young is too important to ignore.

• • •

Volunteer at a suicide prevention phone bank. Help *save* someone's life who is suffering and in deep distress.

Rally behind a local politician.
Ask your friends and neighbors to join you
in getting involved in local politics. Choose a
candidate who will *speak* for you and your
community, and help give a voice to those who
have none and speak for those who can't.

●●●

GIVE UP YOUR WINDOW SEAT.

●●●

Close the worldwide healthcare gap. Support work
being done by organizations such as the Global
Health Council in its work to narrow the gap between
healthcare in developing nations and richer ones.
Of special concern is the health of women and girls for
whom the leading causes of death are HIV/AIDS followed
by malaria, tuberculosis, and pregnancy and childbirth.
Visit www.globalhealth.org for more information.

●●●

Give platelets. It takes a bit longer than donating
blood (around one to two hours) but platelets are an
important part of many lifesaving surgeries.

Buy a cup of
lemonade
from a child's stand.

Support the local police. Make a contribution to the police officers' association charitable foundation in your city. The money usually *supports* widow and orphan groups, college scholarships, youth leagues, drug resistance programs, victim support, and senior programs, among other worthwhile activities.

●●●

Pass on your *reading* material. Take old magazines to a local hospital or a waiting room in a dentist's office.

●●●

SPOIL YOUR PET WITH AN OCCASIONAL TREAT.

●●●

Become a volunteer crossing guard. Some communities rely on volunteers to help kids get home *safely*. Look into volunteering in the morning or afternoon for this important position.

Fight for art classes in schools. It is important for children to learn about the *whole* world and not just their little corner of it. Become an advocate for the children and petition the school board if such a cut happens in your city.

• • •

Give the gift of *sight*. Make a donation to www.sightsavers.org. Your generosity could pay for a cataract operation on an adult to restore his or her sight. A little bit more might buy a microscope for a hospital or train eye care workers. A sizable donation could purchase an all-terrain vehicle for Sightsavers' outreach program providing eye care for people who live in areas with rough terrain.

• • •

Establish a wildlife *refuge* in your garden. All you need to do is supply three things: a protected area where birds can nest, food (living plants as well as seeds, nuts, berries, suet, etc. that you supply), and clean water (birdbath, fountain, etc.). Your little sanctuary will fill with life.

Wave *hello* to
your neighbors.

Lobby a business to change its unfair policies. Start a letter-writing campaign or an email *petition*. Think oil price gouging is going on? Believe our food is unsafe? Want medicines to be more affordable? Align with others in a campaign to get your elected official's attention.

● ● ●

Give a gift from the March of Dimes. Visit the organization's website (www.marchofdimes.com) and browse its merchandise. Choose something that you know a loved one will enjoy and *cherish*. You'll be brightening her day as well as improving the lives of thousands of babies.

● ● ●

Add baking soda to your washer load. This reduces the amount of laundry detergent you will need to use by half, releasing less chemicals into the *environment* every time you do a wash.

● ● ●

Donate bookcases to a school library. Most schools are always looking for small pieces of furniture like bookcases.

Calm a fellow flier's nerves. *Reassure* someone on an airplane with you who fears flying. Do what you can to assuage his fear.

● ● ●

Give a good *reference*. If a coworker is seeking new employment, offer to write a letter of recommendation. Emphasize the skills that individual possesses. Be truthful if the individual had shortcomings that affected his or her work, but don't be disparaging. Separate your emotion from the facts.

● ● ●

Take a child to the zoo. Talk with her about the rich diversity of animal life on our planet. *Explain* each animal's grooming habits, diet, method of bearing young, and natural habitat.

● ● ●

Rescue an injured bird. Sometimes birds fall from their nests or smash into glass windows. In both cases, retrieve the bird (avoid overhandling), place it in a dry box, and *contact* your local animal control center.

Donate a dog or cat bed to an animal shelter. These organizations often have small budgets, so little donations like a bed will go a long way to ensuring at least one animal's *comfort*.

• • •

Volunteer at a local hospital. Volunteers (women and men) serve an *important* function in hospitals that are often understaffed. Volunteers can rock babies to sleep, operate the hospitality cart offering magazines and gum, fetch wheelchairs, and transport discharged patients to their cars.

• • •

Volunteer for the Lesbian, Gay, Bisexual, and Transgender Hotline. Help callers who are struggling with fear, depression, or are in some *kind* of distress as a result of their sexual identity. The hotline number is 1-888-843-4564; visit www.glnh.org for more information.

Establish an insectary in your garden. Special seedlings that attract and support insects *beneficial* to your garden can be planted in a small corner of the space. For example, lupin and sunflowers attract beneficial aphidius that prey upon aphids that are major pests in the garden. It's kind of like companion planting only encouraging an infestation of the right kind of insects.

● ● ●

Learn to perform the Heimlich maneuver. Use it if you see someone choking, unable to cough up food or a foreign object. The simple procedure is easy to learn and could *save* a life. Teach it to your family and friends.

● ● ●

Turn your house *green*. Lend your support to the eco-friendly movement by making your house "green." Install solar panels for heat and utilize rainwater collection and harvesting methods for water. When you renovate or repair your home, use recycled materials as much as possible. Get off the power grid and say goodbye to water bills.

Help an elderly neighbor *clean* her yard. Rake up any leaves, trim her hedges, and mow her lawn. Remove fallen dead tree limbs and brush from her yard. Tree limbs and brush can become a fire danger.

Fight malaria. This *preventable* and curable vector-borne disease kills roughly a million people each year, 90 percent of them children in Africa. Malaria is caused by a parasite that is carried by mosquitoes that infect people. Many of the world's poorest, especially women and children, are at highest risk and once infected have little or no resources to deal with the disease. Find out more at www.malarianomore.org/.

• • •

Be an excellent *witness*. When you observe an accident or criminal activity, stay calm and out of danger. Memorize or take down vital information that would be useful for law enforcement. Share with the police what you have witnessed.

• • •

Register to vote, and vote in every election. You owe it to your country to cast *informed* votes. Recognize it as a privilege and take advantage of it.

Work on behalf of immigrants and illegal aliens. *Advocate* for their humane treatment. Regardless of which side of the law they stand on, they are human beings and deserve fair and just treatment that one member of humanity accords another.

●●●

Remind friends to get their *checkups*. Screenings can detect early breast cancer, colon cancer, prostate problems, heart disease, and a number of other potentially life-threatening illnesses. However, many people put off getting health checkups and screenings. Don't let them.

●●●

Recycle e-waste. Many of the electronics you use in your daily life are harmful to the environment if they are just thrown away. Consider the impact of toxic e-waste in landfills and in the water supply. Make the *choice* to recycle these things instead. Visit www .epa.gov/recycle/electronics-donation-and-recycling to find out more about electronics recycling.

Buy a homeless person a hot meal. It doesn't have to be an expensive sit-down dinner. A hungry person needs nutrition and *nourishment* of the body and soul.

Volunteer at a local hospice organization. You will be *supporting* someone through the process of dying. Each person has to go through the stages of dying alone albeit often surrounded by family, friends, and a support team that will include a hospice nurse and doctor. Find out more at www.hospicenet.org.

● ● ●

Help kids organize a *fundraiser*. One idea is to have a Christmas boutique to raise money for a cause. Kids can paint wooden ornaments, glue on glitter, and tie with string, and then sell them for $1 each.

● ● ●

RETURN YOUR NEIGHBOR'S TRUCK WITH A FULL TANK AFTER BORROWING IT.

● ● ●

Let your boss know that you appreciate her. Perhaps she has great follow-through, comes up with terrific insights, or inspires creativity. Whatever her gift, let her know you admire her. It's probably surprising how infrequently she receives *genuine* admiration from her employees.

Form a "mother of multiples" group. Offer support to others who are sharing similar experiences as parents of multiples. Together you can save money by *sharing* baby clothes and other essentials, trade strategies about raising healthy children, and have play dates for the children when they become old enough for outings at the park and in other people's homes.

● ● ●

Turn off your air conditioner. Once a week during the hot months, *unplug* all the air conditioners in your house. While this may make things warmer than usual, the benefits to the earth's atmosphere (and your electricity bill) are great. Spend the unplugged day outside in the shade.

● ● ●

Teach an arts and crafts class. Contact your local parks and recreation department. There is a need for *interesting* ongoing education that is fun for all ages. It's a good way to share your particular know-how with the school children of your town or city.

Support the work of Orbis in aiding the blind. Out of the thirty-seven million people in the world who are blind, the humanitarian organization Orbis asserts that twenty-eight million of them were blind unnecessarily because of lack of treatment and eye care. Orbis works to *restore* the vision of many in the developing world and prevent blindness. See www.orbis.org.

● ● ●

Keep your neighborhood storm drains *clear*. Rake fallen leaves on the street in front of your home to keep them out of the storm drains. This will prevent flooding on your street during heavy rainstorms.

● ● ●

Volunteer for a mental health hotline. Give support and *comfort* to people in their time of distress.

● ● ●

Become a sponsor to a recovering addict. There are support groups all over the world, and the disease is epidemic. These people need someone to *walk* the steps with them as they are recovering.

Make tiny hats for preemies. Donate these *knitted* caps to your local hospital or a family you know who's recently had a premature baby. Call the hospital neonatal unit to find out if it has rules or criteria for making such items.

●●●

Get involved in community politics. Attend town meetings and help solve local homelessness, panhandling, and other problems that involve the *entire* community.

●●●

Support nonprofit organizations that aid senior citizens and believe in the *importance* of healthy, affordable, and ethical aging services. One such organization is LeadingAge. Visit www .leadingage.org/ for more information.

●●●

Make a donation to The Corps Network. This organization carries on the tradition of the Civilian Conservation Corps in *restoring* the environment. For information on the organization, see www.nascc.org.

Help someone *cross* a busy street. Be it a woman navigating a stroller with other children in tow, an elderly person with a bag of groceries, a child on a bike, a homeless veteran with a shopping cart, or anyone else who looks like he or she could use a little help—offer to help.

Eliminate standing water. Dump out stagnant water in birdbaths, tubs, pots, buckets, and cans on your property. Standing water provides a breeding ground for mosquitoes, which can carry dangerous diseases.

●●●

Recycle batteries instead of throwing them out. Visit www.batteryuniversity.com to learn how to *correctly* dispose of them, and get your office, school, and church involved in their recycling.

●●●

Aid in hurricane disaster relief through organizations such as Direct Relief International. That organization has helped victims of disasters and provides *assistance* to healthcare providers and financially strapped clinics. See www.directrelief.org.

●●●

Help your law enforcement officers *unwind*. Support crime-fighting organizations such as your local chapter of the National Police Athletic/Activities League. Check it out at www.nationalpal.org and make a donation.

Boycott unethical businesses. Refuse to conduct business with those that engage in immoral practices such as using offshore child labor, exploiting workers through low wages and putting them in harm's way, or forcing workers to live in hazardous housing.

• • •

Host a family reunion. *Gather* everyone together and put out long sections of butcher paper and have everyone write out memories and family stories. Make it a day focused around genealogy, family togetherness, and the making of a new tradition.

• • •

Throw a *fundraiser* and donate the proceeds. Solicit a local business to join with you in planning, sponsoring, and hosting a high tea, a black-and-white ball, or a music concert. Donate the money raised to a charity.

• • •

Recycle your old motor oil. Annually, millions of gallons of used oil pollute Earth's waterways. Visit www.recycleoil.org to learn how to properly recycle.

Install a window box
for a neighbor. This simple
act of *kindness* will
brighten up any space.

Help *provide* safe drinking water for children. Water-related diseases are the leading cause of death worldwide. Find and fund programs for safe drinking water.

● ● ●

Host a charity fundraiser for a health-related cause. Whether it's an informal potluck hosted at your house or a black tie event at a fancy restaurant, you can bring your friends, family members, coworkers, and neighbors *together*. Collect donations at the door or charge per plate and then donate all the proceeds to a world health cause.

● ● ●

Purchase some *gifts* for displaced children. Children—whether toddlers, preadolescents, or teenagers—suffer in unimaginable ways when removed from their families and placed in shelters. Visit your local children's shelter. Find out its needs. Help the children placed there in whatever ways you can.

Donate to charitable consignment shops.
De-clutter your house and give unwanted items to
a local thrift store. Some communities have thrift stores
to *benefit* local or global charities.

●●●

NOTIFY NEIGHBORS ABOUT SEVERE WEATHER WARNINGS.

●●●

Support the National Runaway Safeline. Its mission is
to keep kids *safe* who have run away from home, are
thinking about it, or are at-risk. The program also will help
a runaway return home through its Home Free program.
See how you can help at www.1800runaway.org.

●●●

Collect spare change for disaster victims. If everyone
pooled together the loose change (or change cups) that
they find, a *huge* difference could be made for disaster
relief. For help getting organized collecting change, visit
www.changeforchange.org.

Become a volunteer firefighter. Help *support* the first line of defense that protects your community in the case of a fire. Pledge your time, hard work, and willpower to your local volunteer firefighting force. Check out www .nvfc.org for more information on the volunteer force.

●●●

Aid flood-prevention crews. *Join* the sand-bagging team, filling and distributing sandbags before the local river crests and floods outlying areas. Help homeowners board up windows and doors.

●●●

Help a wounded animal. Stop and *call* for aid if you see an animal wounded in a vehicle accident. Contact a local wildlife shelter or emergency veterinarian clinic.

●●●

Take a self-defense class with a family member. Learn how to protect yourself or *defend* someone else.

Give away what's in your closets. Donate unwanted coats, shoes, sweaters, jeans, and other items that you no longer use to a local shelter or charity.

●●●

Help at a local soup kitchen. Don't wait until Thanksgiving or Christmas (when many people volunteer at soup kitchens); find one in your community that needs volunteers and start *now*.

●●●

Rescue disaster-displaced pets. During natural disasters many animals become lost. Keep them *safe* until help arrives or until they can be transported to an animal shelter.

●●●

Support your local battered women's shelter. Donate time, money, or household goods. If the cause is one that speaks to your passion, help any way you can to stop the violence. Call a women's shelter and find out what it specifically needs. Get friends and family to help you *provide* what is needed.

Be a *kinder* parent.
When you show your
child *kindness*, you are
encouraging him or her
to be a nicer person.

Prepare for a disaster. Research online how you and your home can best be *prepared* in the event of a natural disaster.

• • •

Give unused coats and jackets to relief organizations. Put them in a box and donate them in order to *help* people in cold climates survive the cold weather.

• • •

Organize a neighborhood food drive. Get your neighbors to donate canned and nonperishable goods and give them to a local food bank. Make this an event that is not tied to a holiday. Hungry people need food at all times of the year. It's an act of *kindness* at a time when food banks may not be expecting such generosity.

• • •

Help out children who live on the streets. Whether you donate or volunteer, you can give these street youths some choices, skills, and *opportunities* for a better life and healthier future. Check out www.standupforkids.org.

Volunteer to work at the Special Olympics. There are many tasks for volunteers, including *serving* as drivers, athlete escorts, presenters, scorekeepers and timers, fundraisers, coaches, officials, first aid personnel, and more. Click on the "Get Involved" icon at www.specialolympics.org.

• • •

Donate public transit *tickets* to local charity groups. Save your tickets with unused fares remaining on them for organizations that collect the tickets and return them to the transit company for higher-priced tickets. Those are then disseminated to low-income or homeless workers.

• • •

Bring your neighborhood *together*. Rally around a common cause such as beautifying your street or working on a community garden project. Establish a planning committee to arrange for a garden party. Invite everyone in your neighborhood to view the flowers. Serve lemonade and treats. When neighbors know neighbors, they can watch out for each other and their property.

Let the neighborhood kids *play* in your yard.

Support your local film festival. Many cities and even small towns now have film festivals. Become part of the experience by volunteering time or expertise. Many actors in Hollywood were once kids who loved watching films. Be a *force* for bringing film into your community.

● ● ●

Volunteer with Meals on Wheels or another service designed to *bring food* to those with limited mobility. This organization brings meals to elderly people so they do not go hungry. See what you can do to help out the cause by visiting its website at www.mowaa.org.

● ● ●

Help an older relative register her prescriptions *online*. These services are often less expensive and offer door-to-door delivery service.

● ● ●

Offer city workers some water. Next time there is work being done in your neighborhood by city workers, offer them all nice cold glasses of water. It's a great way to *boost* their spirits and productivity.

BUY GROCERIES FOR A FRIEND TIGHT ON CASH.

• • •

Give your mother a "gifts of the self" coupon book. Include coupons for a dinner you will make for her, a spa treatment that you will personally give her, a foot and leg massage with some scented oil, and other ways to spend time showering *love* upon her. Staple your coupons together and present them inside a card. It's perfect for Mother's Day and birthday gifts.

• • •

Volunteer to be the Santa at a children's shelter and bring holiday *cheer* to those who need the most cheering up. Organize a toy drive among your family, friends, and coworkers, and bring a sack of presents with you.

• • •

Help with the after-storm response. *Report* downed power poles, trees, and electrical lines that are casualties of a storm. They pose a dangerous public safety hazard. If you have elderly neighbors, help to clear their yards of fallen branches and other debris once the storm is over.

Welcome new neighbors. Start a committee to greet new families moving into your neighborhood. Make sure everyone takes some time to go over to the new neighbors' house to introduce themselves. Welcome them to their new community of *kindness*!

●●●

Volunteer to be a translator. Whether it is at a school, church, office, or even at the grocery store, your ability to translate and communicate in another language will prove *useful*. Just see the need and fill it.

●●●

Help your family live more *simply*. We collect too much clutter in our lives, buy things we seldom truly need, and suffer from "consumeritis" with its inevitable side effect of credit card debt. So going through and eliminating unnecessary monthly expenditures will help you and your family.

Recommend someone for a local board. Write a letter of introduction for someone you know who seeks to serve on a local community board or charitable foundation.

●●●

Help put an end to childhood poverty. Make a *donation* to an organization such as the National Center for Children in Poverty to help these kids receive the financial support they need. Visit www.nccp.org.

●●●

Participate in a local career day. Volunteer to talk about your career and *inspire* young teens to enter your field of work.

●●●

Support the work of Hesperian Health Guides. The nonprofit publisher produces books about health for people with little formal education. The books are made *available* for distribution within communities where there might not be a doctor or healthcare professional. See www.hesperian.org.

Wash a neighbor's car.
If you already have
everything together to
clean your car, why not
offer to wash your
neighbor's as well?
Have him pull into your
driveway or onto your
lawn and scrub away.

Attend a local school's fundraiser. Whether the school is sponsoring a performance of a well-known play to raise money for the theatrical department or hosting a spaghetti dinner to raise money for the band, *enjoy* an evening at your local school and help the students reach their financial goals.

●●●

Support domestic violence centers. These organizations work on behalf of victims of domestic violence such as the National Center for Children and Families (NCCF). The center not only helps homeless families, but it also provides *services* to neglected and abused children and teens as well as victims of domestic violence. For more information visit www.nccf-cares.org.

●●●

Plan a big family vacation. Invite family members who have moved away. *Invite* aunts, uncles, cousins, grandparents, and great-grandparents. Make the focus less about where you're going and more about who you're going with!

Make a wish come true for a sick child. Youngsters with life-threatening illnesses need the most *hope*. See www.wish.org to see how you can help a child's dreams become reality.

●●●

Volunteer to paint over the graffiti in your city. Help *beautify* your community.

●●●

Mow your neighbor's yard. Invite a lonely neighbor over for coffee. Include that individual in activities involving your friends and family. Sometimes people choose isolation instead of seeking *companionship* because they feel they are intruding in others' lives.

●●●

Volunteer to teach a vocational class at a local shelter. While donations of food and clothing are always helpful, those of the "teach a man to fish" philosophy might consider donating their time and *skill* by teaching a vocational class at a local shelter. This could be anything from job interviewing skills to typing to carpentry.

Donate unused health and beauty items to a women's shelter.

Sort food at a local pantry. After all of the donations come spilling in there needs to be someone there to sort and *organize* everything. A couple of hours can go a long way in a food-sorting facility, making sure that those in need are getting the best of the donations.

● ● ●

D.A.R.E. to keep kids off drugs. The D.A.R.E. program goes into schools and teaches kids not to do drugs. Help out with this *worthy* cause by donating time or money.

● ● ●

Offer to *pick up* food for a neighbor. On your next trip to the grocery store, see if anyone needs anything before you go.

● ● ●

Mentor a local women's group. Share your skills with a woman or group of women. If you feel you don't have the skills, help them find other women who are experts in what they are trying to do or *accomplish*. Find other women willing to be mentors.

Volunteer at a senior citizen center. Offer to teach a workshop on a subject you know well. Such complexes often have a library or a music room or a place where seniors can gather. You will be *sharing* your knowledge with people who maybe can't get out to lectures like they used to, and you may have a captive audience of people intensely interested in your subject.

●●●

Be *prompt* about paying your bills. Maintain a good credit score and nearly every business will want your patronage. Take responsibility for your debt when you incur it.

●●●

Help your elderly relatives organize their medications for the week, making it *easier* for them to know what to take and when. Be cognizant of what medications your parents and grandparents are taking and how often.

Tithe 10 percent of your income. Donate it to your church or favorite local charity. If you have the money and can spare some to put to work for others who have none, then consider making a tithing *commitment*. If your income increases, think about giving more.

● ● ●

Help make a *repair* or do some upkeep at an elderly neighbor's house.

● ● ●

Compliment a family member who has accomplished something. Your *recognition* will likely mean more than any ribbon, badge, certificate, or trophy that he will receive.

● ● ●

Purchase a charitable license plate for your car. Many states have a program where you can show your *support* for different causes on your license plate with a portion of the cost of the plate donated to a charity.

Help a legal immigrant become a citizen. Make sure she understands the requirements for citizenship and help her study for her citizenship test. *Drive* her to take the test or to be sworn in as a citizen of your country.

• • •

Housesit for a friend while she goes on vacation. She will have peace of mind about her home (and possibly pets, if you are watching them as well) and can focus on *enjoying* her vacation.

• • •

See opportunity *everywhere*. We live in an abundant universe. Opportunity isn't something that comes once in a lifetime; it may appear several times a day. Expect it, see it, and seize upon it. It's meant for you. Other people will have their own opportunities.

• • •

Support a fundraiser car wash. While it might not get your car as clean as a professional wash, your *contribution* helps the community.

Crochet items for a
senior care center. Create
lap blankets for elderly
people and donate them to a
local nursing home. Your gifts
will help *warm* their legs
and their hearts.

Set up a companywide *recycling* program.
If your company doesn't have a recycling program in place, work with your operations department to make it happen. Help to get quotes from local recycling plants and see which one would offer your company the best deal.

●●●

Team up with an organization like the Sierra Club (www.sierraclub.org). The reward of seeing the faces of those people whose lives you've *brightened* will be compensation enough.

●●●

Help novice travelers. If you are a seasoned traveler, help someone who is new at it and who may be a little apprehensive. Offer calm *reassurance*. Help them understand the process of checking in, changing planes, disembarking, going through customs, etc.

●●●

Adopt a pet from an animal rescue organization—never buy from a pet store. Do your part and give a loving *home* to a helpless animal.

Support companies that give to charities.
Peruse programs, catalogs, and brochures at
your favorite cultural, charity, or sporting event
for names of sponsors and products to purchase.
Choose to *patronize* those that donate
to your favorite charities.

● ● ●

Give directions to someone who is lost. Keep it simple,
clear, and don't talk too fast. Put a *friendly* face on
your entire community by making the visitor feel welcome
in your town. Give directions and perhaps the name of a
great restaurant nearby or the closest gas station.

● ● ●

Stay at an environmentally conscious hotel or
inn. These are places that are taking that extra step
to *protect* the environment while serving you.
For a full list visit www.greenhotels.com, or if you've
already made a reservation call ahead and ask.

Buy a small gift
for a *friend*,
just because.

Read to kids at a shelter. Call your local homeless or women's shelter and ask if you could come in for one hour each week to *read* to children staying there.

●●●

Help a neighbor paint his house. It's a big job and if the homeowner is trying to do it alone, offer a helping hand. The work will proceed much *faster* with four hands than with two.

●●●

Get your company to *donate* its frequent flyer miles. How many conferences and business trips does your company send you and your coworkers on? See if your bosses would be interested in donating accumulated frequent flyer miles. Several of the airlines will take your miles to help children in need and their families. See sites like www.wish.org and www.fisherhouse.org/programs/hero-miles/ for more information.

●●●

Get an animal ID band or collar for your pet. Consider also having a veterinarian insert an ID chip. These measures can help *recover* a lost pet and help animal rescue services identify animals they find on the streets.

Walk your dog *regularly*. It's an easy task but one that is often overlooked or ignored. Make it a routine daily outing. Your dog will look forward to it and it is healthy for you both.

● ● ●

OPEN YOUR HOME TO THOSE DISPLACED BY DISASTER.

● ● ●

Water your vacationing neighbor's lawn. During a hot spell, turn on his sprinkler or bring yours over to his lawn. *Save* him the effort it takes to replant a burnt lawn.

● ● ●

Put your *extra* change in an expired parking meter. As you're walking through your city center, check and see if anyone is parked at an expired meter. Pop a few coins in. If you have ever received a parking ticket, you probably have wished that someone had done that for you.

Make a wedding album for a recently married friend. Use the pictures you took with your own camera, the wedding invitation, images of the wedding cake, a CD with the song played for the first dance, one of the favors with the new couple's initials on it, and put them all together in an album as a first anniversary gift. Buy scrapbook cutouts, stickers, and fancy papers to add *special* touches or enhance the wedding/marriage theme.

• • •

Talk to your company about *matching* funds. Some companies have a policy that when employees make donations to various charities, they will match the donations.

• • •

Carpool. *Share* your ride to and from work with coworkers. Cutting down on auto emissions and the use of fossil fuels are good things we can do for the planet.

Be a crisis *coach*. If a friend is going through an extremely rough time, call him every evening at a set time to check on how he's doing and to find out if he needs anything or just wants to talk.

●●●

Offer to *pick up* the mail and newspapers. When your neighbor goes on a weekend trip, see if they want you to collect these delivered items. Newspapers piled up in a driveway and mail stuffed into an overfull box signals that no one is home. The house could become a target for burglars.

●●●

Be *kind* to yourself and your baby if you are pregnant. Get prenatal care, take vitamins, eat well, abstain from alcohol, stop smoking, do stretches (such as yoga), exercise (walking and swimming are good), eat well, and do everything in your power to ensure the life you are carrying will come out healthy and strong.

Live by the golden rule.
Treat others with the same
love and *kindness* you
would give yourself and
members of your family.
It's a simple idea but one
that will have a positive
effect on everyone you
come in contact with.

Volunteer at a local animal therapy group. Some places employ animals (for example, horses) in therapy with people in need of *healing*. Set aside some time to help these organizations out by providing some of your time free of charge.

● ● ●

Help a grieving friend. Listen to your heart for inspiration and do what you can to *lighten* that friend's burden. When someone loses a spouse or family member, he or she may shut out others, stop eating, and retreat from the world. Help the grief-stricken person during one of his or her most challenging life transitions. See how it changes your perception of what's important in life.

● ● ●

Be conscious of your behavior when abroad. Represent your home country *proudly* by being courteous and polite.

Listen and learn from your opponents. Be *open* to the ideas of your adversaries and opposites as they might stimulate ideas in you that you may never have conceived without the give-and-take of creative conversation and brainstorming.

●●●

Take *care* of a distressed friend's pet. Offer to brush, feed, walk, or bathe a friend's pet when your friend is in a crisis.

●●●

Make your office an EarthShare workplace. Participants *pledge* a certain amount of each of their paychecks to the cause. Visit www.earthshare.org for more information.

●●●

Keep work at work. Endeavor to keep your career from taking over all the available time in your life. Every life needs *downtime*. Without rest and relaxation your life is out of balance, and you could be neglecting your relationships.

Say "*thank you*" to
your bus driver.

Clean up after your animal. Pick up your dog's poop when you are out walking with him or her. It's mandatory in some communities. Tuck a plastic bag or paper sack into a pocket on your way out for the walk and use it when your dog does his business. If you're feeling extra *kind*, pick up after someone else's dog too.

● ● ●

Remain calm. Practice patience, *kindness*, and serenity by counting to ten or following the breath in and out. Such practices help to provide a counterbalance to the effects of daily stress.

● ● ●

Be *mindful* of competitors. Strive to be the best but don't bring down someone else to get to the top. Personal gain is nothing if accomplished at a cost to others.

● ● ●

Notice the good and offer *praise*. If you notice a coworker is remarkable in some way, take the time to tell that person. It will make that person's day and help your coworker to be more productive.

Build or buy a birdfeeder. After filling it, remember to regularly clean it to avoid spread of avian infections. If you fill your feeder with bird food that *attracts* songbirds, you'll enjoy listening to the songs of your newly found feathered friends.

●●●

Say "no thanks" to fresh linens daily. Some hotels have a system where only towels left on the floor will be replaced with new ones. You'll do the environment a *favor* by reusing.

●●●

Save electricity and dine al fresco. On a warm evening set up a table in the garden, courtyard, or backyard. Burn citronella to keep the mosquitoes away. Make the table pretty, dressing it up with special linen, china, and flatware. Prepare a special meal with the freshest ingredients and serve it with a fine bottle of wine. Enjoy the *company* of your friends and family, or just enjoy being on your own.

Be a *support* person for a caregiver. A caregiver's life is filled with hard labor and emotional ups and downs that can take a devastating toll on her health. Being a support person for a caregiver is one of the most important roles you can fulfill.

● ● ●

Practice yoga with someone you care about. The emphasis is on relaxing into peace, attuning to the body's wisdom and guidance, and establishing the time and means for relaxation, strengthening, and *healing* to occur.

● ● ●

Take *time* to meditate each day. You may only have five minutes to spare, but take it for yourself. Turn within. Tune out the world and your five senses. Sink deep into the quiet and deepest place of Self and feel the inner peace.

● ● ●

Organize a neighborhood open forum. Start an informal discussion group to air neighborhood issues of concern. Focus on constructive problem-solving. Without alienating anyone or discounting any neighbor's ideas, *engage* in vigorous debate and explore all possible solutions.

Make holiday cards *green*. Encourage your office to send a holiday e-card this year rather than wasting paper by mailing out paper greeting cards.

●●●

Eat less meat. On average it costs much more to raise a herd of animals (feed, supplements, land, shelter, veterinarian costs, etc.) than to raise a field of beans or corn or produce other nonanimal sources of protein. Eating less meat is a *good* thing to do for your body and the planet.

●●●

Protect your child against skin cancer. Caused by the sun's harmful ultraviolet rays, it can be *prevented* by making sure he wears a wide-brimmed hat and is covered with a good sunscreen with an SPF rating of at least 15 over exposed parts of his body before going outdoors.

Give money to a friend. Drop an *extra* $20 bill into an envelope and send it anonymously to a friend of a friend who is struggling to make ends meet.

Give a loved one a foot massage. Don't do it because you expect one in return; do it because you want to help your loved one *relax*.

●●●

Support local chapters of women's business organizations. These organizations *help* career-minded women and women-owned businesses thrive and prosper. Most groups offer lectures, networking, and informational events, and they promote economic alliances. They trade information, build strategic alliances, and effect policy changes that affect women-owned businesses. Find a chapter near you by searching online.

●●●

Create a *healthier* work environment. Ask your manager or boss to monitor the air quality where you and your coworkers spend the greatest part of your workday. Chemical contaminants in the environment can make people sick. Worse, they can lead to permanent health issues causing lower productivity and higher medical expenses.

Help a coworker think *creatively*. Sometimes it's easier to think outside the box with another person. The next time he meets a roadblock in his career path, sit with him and discuss possible solutions to his problem. Two heads coming up with a variety of ideas on how to navigate such impediments can be better than one.

● ● ●

Stop being habitually critical and negative. It spreads like a disease, infecting everyone in your office with whom you have contact. Don't just break the bad habit; replace it with a good habit that includes lots of positive thinking and words of *kindness* for those with whom you work.

● ● ●

Report suspicious behavior. Pay *attention* to who is around you, whether sitting on a plane, in an airport, on a subway, or at a crowded event. A heightened awareness is a good thing to have in today's world.

Take your cat or dog to a senior center for a visit. Animals have a therapeutic *healing* effect on people. Call ahead for permission, and then take your well-behaved pet to a nursing home for a visit with the residents. Watch how your pet cheers up young and old alike.

OFFER TO BABYSIT A FRIEND'S CHILDREN FOR FREE.

● ● ●

Help a coworker unload boxes of office supplies. Carrying in boxes of paper, toner cartridges, pens and pencils, paper clips, and the stuff that keeps offices running can be drudgery, but a *helping* hand makes it go faster.

● ● ●

Refill the copier's paper tray. This *simple* act will save someone else time when she goes to make copies and doesn't have to worry about being out of paper.

● ● ●

Buy from local businesses when you travel. Doing so means you are supporting a local economy. Buy *original* art from artisans painting in a lane in France, bread from a boy with loaves on his bike in a Russian village, or scroll paintings from monks in Nepal.

Learn how to give *positive* criticism and feedback. Giving and receiving criticism is not easy. Finding fault is easy, but finding fault isn't the point. Offer honest criticism in private. Be calm and thoughtful when making your point. Show a spirit of concern and a desire to help. If it's a project that is the focus of the criticism, explain what isn't working and why. Focus on the problem, not the person. Offer suggestions for fixing the problem or making the project better. Solicit feedback to make sure the other person understands the point you are making.

●●●

Invest in socially *responsible* mutual funds. It's a way to do social good while putting your money to work for you. Ask your investment banker or counselor for input and suggestions for ones that factor in your level of risk.

Be a foster *caregiver* to an abandoned animal.
If you cannot adopt but you could provide interim
shelter, food, and veterinarian care for a helpless animal,
consider being a foster care provider.

● ● ●

Establish five *charitable* goals for
your company. Set a list of priorities for giving
this year and get your company involved in
helping achieve these generous acts. Spread
your generosity out among different groups
and organizations.

● ● ●

Step aside for those with connecting flights.
Let someone cut in front of you if she has to make
a connecting flight and you don't. Sometimes to get from
one flight to another or to change airlines you have to
get off the plane and literally run to another gate.
Missing a connection is a major headache.

Put up fliers for a lost pet. The time you spend helping to find the lost animal will benefit both pet and owner. Make a difference by donating your time and commitment to helping to bring that animal *home*.

● ● ●

Be a courteous driver. *Resist* the urge to express road rage when a tense driving situation calls forth such urges. Instead of giving inconsiderate drivers the finger, slamming on your horn, yelling at your kids, or chewing out an employee when you get to work or the person who nabs the parking spot in front of you, count to ten and breathe deeply. Redirect the urge to lash out by counting and breathing deeply.

● ● ●

Brush your pet's teeth. Oral health is as *important* for your animals as it is for you. Insist on dental health checkups at your pet's regular veterinarian visit.

Practice good
cell phone *etiquette*.
When you're in a public
place, put your phone on
vibrate setting and return
missed calls in a more
private environment.

Buy shatter-resistant sunglasses for your children. Children spend more time outside in the sun than adults do, so parents need to pay attention to their children's vision and schedule regular eye exams. You need to *protect* their eyes against harmful ultraviolet rays.

• • •

Be *kind* to yourself about your appearance. Many people hold unrealistic ideals about what their body should look like. The shape and appearance of each body is dependent on many factors, including genes. Plastic surgery increasingly is a choice some people make to achieve a body image they desire. But surgery carries with it many risks. Be well informed.

• • •

Donate a cat carrier to an animal shelter. The carriers come in *handy* when transporting cats, and animal rescue organizations are always looking for ones in good condition. Or you could give it to a cat owner you know but who doesn't have the financial means to purchase one.

Buy fresh fruits and vegetables in bulk.
Not only will you be helping your family eat healthier and
supporting local farmers, but you'll also be saving
some pennies. Packaging cost is carefully calculated into
the price of the product. You didn't think you were getting
it free, did you? Not only do you have to pay for it, you
have to recycle or otherwise dispose of it.

● ● ●

Dust for someone with dust allergies or
mow the lawn for someone with outdoor
allergies. These *small* chores can mean big
trouble for allergy sufferers!

● ● ●

Build a support network. Stuck is the worst place
to be, both physically and psychologically. Creating a
network of *kindhearted* friends that each of you
can reach out to when times get rough ensures that you
will all be able to carry on and move forward.

Choose *kindness*.
The next time you open
your mouth to share a
piece of gossip or hurl
an insult, instead offer a
compliment to a friend,
family member,
or stranger.

Give dark chocolate. Once in a while a piece of dark chocolate is just what is needed to *lift* a mood or satisfy a craving. Dark chocolate contains flavonoids, compounds with antioxidants that inhibit or slow down damage to the body by free radicals (unstable oxygen molecules that harm cell structures). So next time you buy someone a box of chocolates, go for dark chocolate.

●●●

Do not judge others. Try to *understand* them. It is much better to judge yourself and change what you do not like after a period of honest introspection.

●●●

Don't spread your cold! Colds are caused by a family of more than two hundred different viruses. You can spread your cold by simply shaking someone's hand. If you have a cold, *wash* your hands frequently and cover your mouth with the crook of your arm (not your hand) when you cough.

Buy cough drops for a sick coworker. When you have a cold, that *kindness* is extra appreciated!

●●●

Buckle up. Every time you get behind the wheel make sure those you are driving put on their *seatbelts*. Wearing seatbelts saves lives.

●●●

Be a *generous* listener. All too often we tell others all about ourselves. In fact, most of us would rather the conversation be all about us most of the time. Resist the urge to make it be all about you. Take the time to really get to know someone else. Ask lots of questions.

●●●

Give gifts. Bombard the love of your life with tokens of affection and appreciation—from thoughtful notes (you later can put these in a scrapbook about your life together) to intimate dinners and pillow talk. Resist taking each other for granted and instead *celebrate* your love.

Coach a children's sports team. If you don't
know how to play the particular sport, volunteer to help
the coach and do whatever is needed. *Demonstrate*
good sportsmanship on the ball field, ice rink, or
gymnastics floor.

● ● ●

Help your friend with her business.
Help redesign her website, review her pricing,
or make staff recommendations. Whatever
your special skill is, *offer* it to your
friend, free of charge.

● ● ●

Encourage a loved one in pain to get help
or counseling. Find a *caring* way to tell him that
what he is doing is wrong and hurtful to himself
and others. Set firm boundaries to protect yourself
in the event he turns his hostility upon you.

Use biodegradable bags. Be *kind* to the earth and pick up some earth-friendly bags the next time you're at PetCo or other pet stores. Choosing to clean up after your pet's mess with something like BioBag—100 percent biodegradable dog waste bags—will help the environment and your neighborhood.

●●●

Pack a first aid kit for your family. Find out what goes into a home first aid kit and put one together for your family. Your *preparation* could save someone from serious injury. Start by checking out the info on WebMD at www .emedicinehealth.com/first_aid_kits/topic-guide.htm.

●●●

Raise awareness about spaying and neutering. Spaying and neutering animals reduces the growing populations of stray dogs and cats and can have an added *benefit* of reducing the incidents of humans being bitten by such animals infected with rabies or other diseases.

Brighten up your workplace. Hang art, photos of coworkers, or inspirational sayings you found on Pinterest.

Write a love *poem*. Tell your lover how much he means to you in verse. Leave it on his pillow along with a chocolate and an IOU for a massage when your schedules permit.

●●●

Create a going-away present as a family. Involve your entire family in making individual quilt squares to *honor* someone moving away. Each square could demonstrate some way that person was important in your life. Sew the squares together. Add a border and a backing.

●●●

Help your parents stave off dementia. The best way to avoid age-related dementia is through *learning*. Teach them how to play the violin, encourage them to learn a new language, or start playing mahjong or chess with them.

Believe in second *chances*. Open
yourself to infinite possibilities in relationships,
love, and happiness. Second, third, and fourth
chances do come around.

● ● ●

Learn sign language and then
embrace the opportunity to communicate
with your nonhearing friends.

● ● ●

Return phone calls and emails promptly. It shows respect
and *kindness* for the caller and writer.

● ● ●

Teach a child to cook. Make sure the project is
age appropriate and the child's safety is ensured.
Make it fun and easy. Cooking together will
instill *confidence* in the child and provide
a way for you to spend quality time together.

Be courteous and *kind*

to those serving you.

Set out a bowl of candy for everyone
in the office to *share*.

●●●

SURPRISE YOUR LOVER WITH BREAKFAST IN BED.

●●●

Encourage a friend to exercise and diet
with you. *Reinforce* each other's efforts to get
healthy and stay that way. Sometimes the hardest
part of staying healthy is doing it alone.

●●●

Make a donation to an animal sterilization clinic.
Look into organizations like Spay Neuter Assistance
Program (SNAP) or the American Society for the
Prevention of Cruelty to Animals (ASPCA). Through spay/
neuter clinics on wheels, such organizations usually offer
services free or at reduced fees to low-income families
receiving public assistance such as food stamps. To find
out more go to www.spayusa.org or www.aspca.org.

Give a massage. Nothing promotes the sense of healing and nurturing as the human *touch*. We all need it. So offer a massage to a friend. If you don't think you can give a good enough one, then pay for a massage. Many spas offer a variety of types such as Japanese, Swedish, Ayurvedic, and myriad others. Some include aromatherapy and a hot presoak before the massage.

● ● ●

Pick a friend up at the airport. This is especially *kind* if her flight comes in late at night or early in the morning. She likely will feel exhausted and possibly not as alert as she would normally be to drive herself home or deal with hailing a taxi or catching a shuttle. Besides, for her, having a friend or family member pick her up after a trip makes the last leg of the journey much more tolerable and less stressful.

Inspire the love of theater in children.
Establish a children's theater group in your community,
either through a parks and recreation department, a local
school, or on your own with help from other parents.
Involve the children in every aspect, from making
costumes to painting sets and acting. It exposes them
to potential career paths while encouraging
teamwork and self-expression.

●●●

Aid in the rescue of parrots and
parakeets. Make a donation to a bird-specific aid
organization or sanctuary. For more information
go to www.the-oasis.org and make a donation.

●●●

Write a children's story about your kid. Whether
it's an action adventure in which your child saves the day
or a fairy tale where she lives happily ever after, she will
be *captivated* by it and love that you took the time
to write it. This is an especially good gift for a birthday.

Volunteer to work at a local animal *shelter*. Let the organization know about any special skills or expertise you have such as editing a newsletter, designing a radio/TV ad campaign, or brainstorming fundraising ideas. See www.hsus.org and learn how you can help the cause.

● ● ●

Help your family go *paperless*. Try to get important records, schedules, and calendars of school activities and family events onto the computer. The less paper you use as a household, the more you're helping the environment.

● ● ●

DONATE A FIRST AID KIT TO A WOMEN'S SHELTER.

● ● ●

Buy your child a toy for *no reason*. When you give it to him, ask that he pick out one of his own gently used toys, books, or games to donate to a charity, toy drive, or library.

Focus on seeing things
for what they are. Develop
the attitude that you must
try to see things and people
as they *truly* are, not as
you wish them to be.

Bring the joy of animals to at-risk youth. Volunteer to work with an organization that offers the *healing* touch of animals to those children and teens who need it the most. Check out programs like those run through the Gentle Barn (www.gentlebarn.org).

●●●

Invite your partner out for a wild afternoon. Take him to the zoo. Learn about the animals and make a donation to *support* their care and feeding.

●●●

Promote healthy living. Make sure your family is not only eating and exercising well but is in a good state of mental health. Talk to them. Cheer them up. Get them to discuss their feelings. Offer to help with a friend's wedding. It can be overwhelming, and an extra pair of hands and eyes may be just what the family needs. Whether it's running simple errands or helping set up the event hall, your *kindness* will be appreciated.

Be there to do the small things on moving day. Moving day is a hectic time, so *be there* for your friend. Offer to do a run to a local coffee shop since she probably doesn't have the time to make a pot of java. Provide encouraging words as she may be feeling a little overwhelmed. Help her focus on what needs to be done, be there at the end to support her, and know that strong friendships can be sustained across many miles and over lifetimes.

● ● ●

Compliment your partner's inner beauty. Appreciate her *kindness*, grace, intelligence, humor, and generosity—all sexy and sought-after attributes far better and longer lasting than a facial, manicure, and haircut. Inner beauty is more attractive and longer lasting than physical appearance.

Start a book club
and discussion group.
A book club is a great way
for people to *share* their
love of reading, build a
sense of community, and
make friends.

Remain positive. Don't be defeatist. Accept that you are someone unique (because you are). There is no one else exactly like you in the world; even identical twins or multiples have some differences. Celebrate your gifts and talents. Focus on them rather than what you lack. You are here for a reason, so be *kind* to yourself!

● ● ●

Know when not to involve yourself.
Recognize when someone in crisis does not want your help and *respect* her position. It is one of the hardest things to do. Our impulse is to rush in and fix the problem. But we have to remember it is her crisis, not ours. We must honor her desire to figure things out alone.

● ● ●

READ TO YOUR CHILDREN.

Think positively. When you imagine *wonderful* things in your life, imagine equally wonderful things manifesting in the lives of others.

● ● ●

Don't worry. Replace worry with positive *affirmations* and a strong and clear mental image of what you want manifested in your life. Use your will yoked with a positive course of action to make it happen.

● ● ●

Take the whole family on a weekend outing. A short trip to a local strawberry patch or an apple orchard can be fun for the kids and relaxing for the parents. When the entire family *participates* in frequent outings, it brings everyone closer together and reduces the tensions that have built up during the week.

Do something new with your partner. Psychologists say *sharing* novel experiences can deepen your happiness.

• • •

Keep children and teens *busy* with fun activities. Volunteer at after-school clubs, camps, church events, and service projects. A youngster with too much time and nothing to do is more likely to get into trouble than a child who has an active social life.

• • •

Donate used household electronics to charities. Box up old fax machines, monitors, computers, televisions, radios, and cell phones that your family no longer uses and give them to worthwhile causes. They are always looking for *functioning* equipment that is in good shape.

Knit something for a new addition. If you've recently added a new member to your immediate or extended family, make some booties, a sweater, or a hat for the new baby. These types of *personally* crafted gifts truly come from the heart and will be appreciated and cherished by the parents.

●●●

Be *kind* to your skin. If it is dry and cracked, fill a tub full of warm to hot water and pour in a few capfuls of body oil. Get into the tub and lie on your back, then stomach, then back again. Massage the oil into your skin. When you get out of the tub, take care not to slip. Continue rubbing in the oil all over and then pat your skin dry. The fine lines and cracks will have disappeared.

●●●

Don't let anyone drive under the influence. If you are out with a friend who has had too much to drink, *call* him a taxi or get him an Uber, then help him retrieve his car in the morning.

Do a friend's dishes. Clear and do the dishes the next time you have dinner at a friend's, neighbor's, or acquaintance's house. It shows good *manners* and is a great way to thank her for having you over.

Take a class and learn about conflict *resolution*. Apply it to the relationships in your life and watch how the causes of conflicts begin to shift or diminish.

●●●

Swap skills with a friend. Offer to teach a friend how to make killer guacamole if he will show you how to irrigate your lawn. You both benefit from sharing your *knowledge* with each other.

●●●

Strive for equality in your love relationship. Relationships in which the couples share *equally* in sacrifices, decision-making, communication, and chores are more likely to succeed than those relationships in which one person dominates the other.

Plan a children's tea *party*. Invite bears, dolls, and other stuffed animals. Wear fancy hats. Allow the children to set the table with napkins, spoons, and teacups. Add a plate of sandwiches and jar of gingersnaps. The children will love it.

● ● ●

Help a friend who wants to learn to cook. Buy him new pans or donate your old ones and one of your cookbooks. Don't do it because he might reward you with a gourmet meal; do it because it will give him such *joy* to have the necessary tools to start cooking.

● ● ●

Plant some perennials in a cancer patient's garden. Put them where he can see them blooming. Annuals die each year and must be replaced, but perennials return year after year. Your gesture is a small, unspoken statement of your *hope*.

Pay for the person behind you. Next time you pull up to the drive-thru window pay for what you ordered and what the person behind you ordered. When it's his turn to pay he'll be pleasantly surprised by your *kind* act.

Boycott unregulated foreign products.
These companies can have harsh regimes. In particular
do not support products coming from places where
governments exploit their own people, force people to
work in unsafe conditions, and sustain control of power
through threats of violence or imprisonment.

● ● ●

**Find the greater *good* in every
moment. Learn from the stressful and
negative experiences but put your energy into
finding the silver lining, seeing the good,
and praising it.**

● ● ●

Carry a piece of *luggage* for a stranger.
Help an elderly person or parent with a stroller
carry large pieces of luggage. Chances are she has
been toting those big bags around for a while
now and could use the help.

Expand your horizons. Take a lifelong learning trip. Offered through universities, you can go on an archeological dig, an Audubon expedition, a history excursion, or myriad other adventures, often with a college professor as your guide and guest lecturer.

● ● ●

Truly listen to your partner's joys and concerns. Take time out to *listen*, even just about the events of the day. Make sure you're actually listening and not interrupting with your own stories.

● ● ●

Let someone have the taxi you've just hailed. Next time you hail a cab while it's busy on the street, let the person standing next to you have it. This *simple gesture* may cost a few minutes of your time, but it will mean the world to the stranger you helped.

Allow someone to go out in front of you from the elevator. Don't rush in front of people the next time you exit an elevator. Let the other occupants get out *before* you go on with your day.

● ● ●

Help a child learn about investing. Start with the financial basics: earning, saving, and finding ways to make the money grow. What better way to help a young person *develop* some real-world skills that will serve him throughout life.

● ● ●

Write your lover a *love* letter. Fill it with your thoughts of a strong and deep inner passion.

● ● ●

Help a friend with her yard sale. Having items already sorted, in labeled boxes, and marked with prices on stickers or tags makes it *easier* to move the merchandise because buyers don't have to ask the prices.

Make a *dream* come true for an ill child. Become a volunteer at your local chapter of Dream Factory, an organization that works with volunteers, nonprofit organizations, and corporations to procure dreams for children who suffer from a life-threatening illness. Find out more at www.dreamfactoryinc.org.

● ● ●

Open a door for someone carrying packages. This little extra *effort* will help prevent any tumbling and breaking.

● ● ●

Return lost items. Don't just assume someone else will do it. Immediately *return* a found wallet, money, or other item that someone has dropped or left behind. Your decision to help out could have a huge impact on someone else's life.

● ● ●

Mop with white vinegar and water. Next time you need to *clean* your linoleum floors, don't use expensive floor cleaning supplies. These may contain unduly harsh or toxic ingredients.

Hold the elevator door
for someone.

Be thankful for the gift of your life.
It's nothing short of miraculous to be in the
world. We are equipped with special talents
and gifts to help us in life. These are the best
kind of possessions, ones for which we
ought to be grateful.

● ● ●

Help someone out at the grocery store.
Reach *high* to retrieve a grocery item for
someone who wants it but can't reach it. If
neither of you can reach it, offer to get help.

● ● ●

Give up your seat on a bus. Whether it's to an elderly
person, a pregnant woman, a young mother with several
children, a physically challenged person, or someone who
simply looks weary, giving your seat up will help that
person out and *brighten* his or her day.

Be punctual. Don't make your friends wait.
Show them that you *respect* their time. When
you agree to meet for socializing, don't be late. Chronic
lateness suggests many negatives: you don't care, you
don't know how to budget time, you are a procrastinator,
or you are careless and do not pay attention to details
(like knowing what time it is).

●●●

Don't talk about stress; do something about it. Break the
cycle of complaining about your high stress level. It's
giving mental energy to bringing more of it your way.
Instead focus on how you can *de-stress* your life.

●●●

Pay back any money that you owe, be it to
a family member, a friend, or a business colleague.
Make the *effort* to do the right thing, even if you
can afford to make only small payments.

Overtip a good waiter
or waitress.

Stop being competitive. Let go of competition with your lover or spouse over who earns the most money. In the grand scheme of things it really doesn't matter, does it? Just count your *blessings* that you both can contribute to your income.

●●●

Help someone change a flat tire, even if it's raining. If you've ever had to *change a flat tire* on your own before, you know how much of a hassle it can be. So next time you see someone changing a tire on the side of the road, pull over and offer an extra hand—even if it's just to hold an umbrella over someone's head.

●●●

Pull all the way *forward* at the gas pump. This way the car following can use the pump behind you. Otherwise, that driver will have to wait until you finish pumping your gas, find another pump, or do tricky maneuvering to get into a position elsewhere at the station.

Forgive. Priests, psychologists, and doctors know that the act of forgiveness helps heal a person's body as well as heart, mind, and soul. You may think forgiving helps the other person, but, in fact, it helps you both.

• • •

Be *sincere*. Be brave enough to speak openly from your heart to your friends when they seek your opinion. Don't be duplicitous, telling them one thing to their face and something different behind their backs. Your friends will appreciate your sincerity, and you will begin to feel honor bound to tell the truth.

• • •

Empty your pantry for a young relative's first house. Buying a home is a big step. *Filling* the kitchen cupboards with food is an additional expense at a time when it may seem to her that the cash register has been constantly ringing. Help a young relative by filling her cupboards for her.

Allow your friends to *pay* you back in other ways. If a friend is strapped for cash and you've loaned him some money, let him do something for you rather than actually paying you back. Instead of giving you money, he could cook dinner for you both or give you a ride to the airport.

●●●

Take a break from fast food. Be *kind* to your body and reacquaint yourself, your family, and friends with the pleasure of taking time to prepare a great meal from the freshest and highest-quality ingredients. You'll be giving a gift to yourself as well as to others.

●●●

Be a true *friend*. Don't be someone who uses friends to constantly complain, spread gossip, or backstab others. Friendships won't last if bathed in an environment of resentment, anger, or self-pity. There's truth in the old expression, "To have a friend, you must be a friend."

Invite a neighbor's children to the movies with yours. It'll heighten your youngsters' enjoyment of their afternoon outing. Although your neighbor may reciprocate—ensuring your own child-free afternoon—don't expect or count on it. Do your good deed and know that you made it possible for a group of kids to have a *wonderful* day.

● ● ●

Remember *single* friends during special times. Keep your friend who is single and without family in mind on his birthday and at other holiday times during the year. Invite him to celebratory dinners, send him birthday greetings (even if it is just an email card), and introduce him to your other single friends. Your efforts of inclusion might mean his support network will grow.

● ● ●

Make sure your mother and aunts get *regular* mammograms. Early detection of breast cancer saves lives. See www .center4research.org for more information.

Keep your friend's glass half full. Be an *optimist* and try to have her see the best-case scenario rather than its opposite. Whether it is love, health, finances, or a job issue that she's worrying about, help her let it go, relax, and let in the good.

Keep your promises. Follow through whenever you give your word. If you make a *promise* to someone and then forget about it ten minutes later, that lack of attention to follow through violates any trust you may have established. Remember what you promised to do and then do it.

● ● ●

Speak out against hateful comments. When you hear slurs or epithets hurled at someone, *stand up* for that person. Refuse to be complicit in the act by your inaction. Call law enforcement if the person is threatened or the situation deteriorates. Do something. Apathy is bad karma.

● ● ●

Cut the plastic rings of any six-pack beverage carrier. Those plastic holders make it into the ocean where they are harmful to dolphins and other sea life.

Handle conflicts without negative confrontations. Find new words that are neutral as opposed to inflammatory language to clearly and precisely express difficult feelings toward loved ones, business associates, or coworkers. Avoid bringing up past conversations, situations, or events that might trigger a defensive, hostile, or aggressive act toward you. Try to remain calm even as you explain the problem and endeavor to establish *boundaries* for self-preservation. Doing something good for yourself like establishing limits or boundaries is of primary importance.

●●●

Have your friends buy *local* produce. Get them together for a weekend of fruit picking from local orchards. When you've plucked all the bounty from the trees, take a few boxes or bags of the fruit to a local food bank or homeless shelter.

Keep a secret.
When a friend, relative, child,
or business associate tells
you something in confidence,
do your utmost to *honor*
that person by keeping
a secret.

Lobby for *free* rides for the homeless.
Petition your community public transportation
officials to provide free rides to the homeless
who use public transportation.

●●●

Send a care package to your child in college.
When your college-age daughter becomes frustrated or a
little depressed during her final examinations, make her a
special basket. Put in scented oils, mini French-milled
soaps, mint lotion for the feet, pumice, nail clippers, a bag
of chamomile tea, and a CD of beautiful relaxing music.

●●●

Give the gift of separation. Allow for some time apart
from your loved one to *appreciate* your relationship.
Love depends more on the quality of time spent together
rather than the amount of time. Time apart can be healthy
and good for a romantic relationship.

●●●

Volunteer to be a mentor to a child.
Your commitment could have a *positive*
impact on the life of a young person.

Be *responsible* about your finances.
Try not to spend money you don't have.
Keep track of your credit card debt and pay
off the entire bill if you can every billing cycle.

● ● ●

Help *fix up* a friend's home before she sells it.
You might pack boxes, wrap pictures and paintings in
brown paper for shipping, put outdated documents
through a shredder so they don't have to be part of the
move, clean out the garage so excess furniture can be
put there when the new carpet goes in, or go through
the house with spackle and a trowel to patch small
nail holes in preparation for the painters.

● ● ●

Cook a meal for a relative with a new baby. After the
birth of a baby, everyone's so busy there's hardly any
time to eat. Help out the family by putting together a
homemade dinner and delivering it to their home.

Learn cardiopulmonary resuscitation (CPR). Your knowledge and fast *action* could save someone's life. Courses are offered through community colleges, parks and recreation departments, and local branches of the Red Cross. You can even learn CPR from a video that has been approved by the American Heart Association. Check out www.cpr-training-classes.com to sign up.

●●●

Return *kind* gestures. If a friend brings you a basket of bounty from her yard or a plate with a homemade treat, respond in kind. When the basket or plate is empty, put fruit or vegetables in the basket and cookies or a slice of homemade pie or cake on the plate before returning the basket or dish to its owner.

●●●

Reward yourself. Every time you hit a milestone in a big project, give yourself a *treat*. Sometimes just knowing there's a little reward waiting is enough of an impetus to keep you on track.

Join the effort to find a cure for an incurable disease or disability. There are many from which to choose, including HIV/AIDS, many types of cancer, multiple sclerosis, autism, cystic fibrosis, polio, and Tay-Sachs. Research how you can help. Now make that cause your *mission*. Get off the couch, out of the house, and make your life count in the effort to save someone else's life.

● ● ●

Speak *kindly*. If people around you are complaining about life, listen compassionately to their complaints and acknowledge the suffering they are feeling, but don't feed it.

● ● ●

Admit when you're wrong. Go to the person involved and apologize. It will make that person feel *validated*, and you will generate good karma as you learn from your mistake.

● ● ●

Make chicken soup for an ill family member. It soothes sore throats in people with colds and the flu, and its anti-inflammatory agents may *boost* the immune system.

Balance unkindness
with acts of *kindness*.
If the person in the line
ahead of you at the bank
snaps meanly at the
teller, shift the energy.
When it is your turn,
say something to
lift her spirits.